Intervention
Annotated Teacher's Edition

Level 1

SRA

Columbus, OH

Send all inquiries to this address:
SRA/McGraw-Hill
4400 Easton Commons
Columbus, OH 43219

ISBN: 978-0-07-610413-0
MHID: 0-07-610413-3

3 4 5 6 7 8 9 COU 13 12 11 10 09 08 07

The *McGraw·Hill* Companies

Intervention

Unit 1 Back to School

Unit 2 Where Animals Live

Unit 3 I Am Responsible!

Unit 4 Our Neighborhood at Work

Table of Contents

Unit 5 What's the Weather?

Unit 6 North, South, East, West

Unit 7 I Think I Can

Unit 8 Away We Grow!

Table of Contents

Unit 9 Home, Sweet Home

Unit 10 I Am Brave

Name _____ **Date** _____

Name each picture. If students hear the /s/ sound in the picture name, they should circle the picture. Tell them that /s/ can come at the beginning or the end.

Name _____ **Date** _____

Name each picture. If students hear the /m/ sound in the picture name, they should circle the picture. Tell them that /m/ can come at the beginning or the end.

Name _____ Date _____

Name each picture. Have students circle the pictures whose names begin with the /a/ sound.

Name _____ Date _____

Name each picture. If students hear the /t/ sound in the picture name, they should circle the picture. Tell them that /t/ can come at the beginning or the end.

Name _____ Date _____

Part 1 Name each picture. Have students circle the letter that stands for the beginning sound in the word.

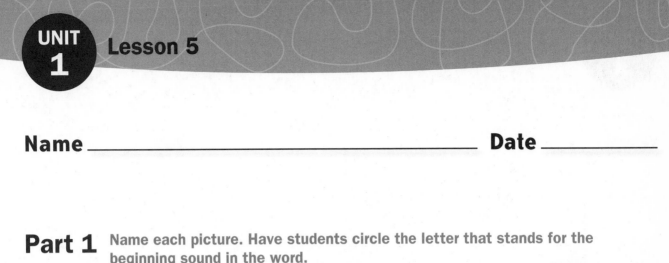

s m a(t) s m a(t) (s)m a t

s m a(t) s(m)a t (s)m a t

Part 2 Name each picture. Have students circle the letter that stands for the ending sound in the word.

s m a(t) s(m)a t (s)m a t

Name _____ Date _____

Name each picture. If students hear the /d/ sound in the picture name, they should circle the picture. Tell them that /d/ can come at the beginning or the end.

Name _____ **Date** _____

Name each picture. If students hear the /n/ sound in the picture name, they should circle the picture. Tell them that /n/ can come at the beginning or the end.

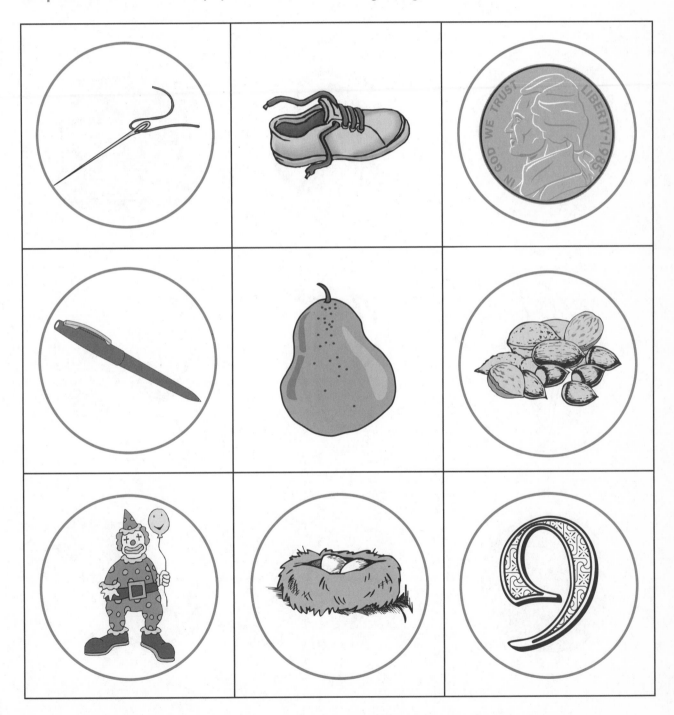

Name _____ Date _____

Say the word that names each picture. Have students circle the pictures whose names have the /i/ sound.

Intervention

Name _____ **Date** _____

Name each picture. If students hear the /h/ sound in the picture name, they should circle the picture. Tell them that /h/ comes at the beginning.

Name _____ **Date** _____

Read the sentences. Have students circle the nouns in each sentence.

1. My (friend) has a new (kitten.)

2. The (kitten) is cute and furry.

3. It plays with (string) on the (floor.)

4. It chases its (tail.)

5. It curls up in a (basket.)

6. It sleeps on a soft (bed) in my (bedroom.)

7. The (kitten) has black (whiskers.)

8. It has a gray (spot) on its (head.)

Name _____ **Date** _____

Name each picture. If students hear the /p/ sound in the picture name, they should circle the picture. Tell them that /p/ can come at the beginning or the end.

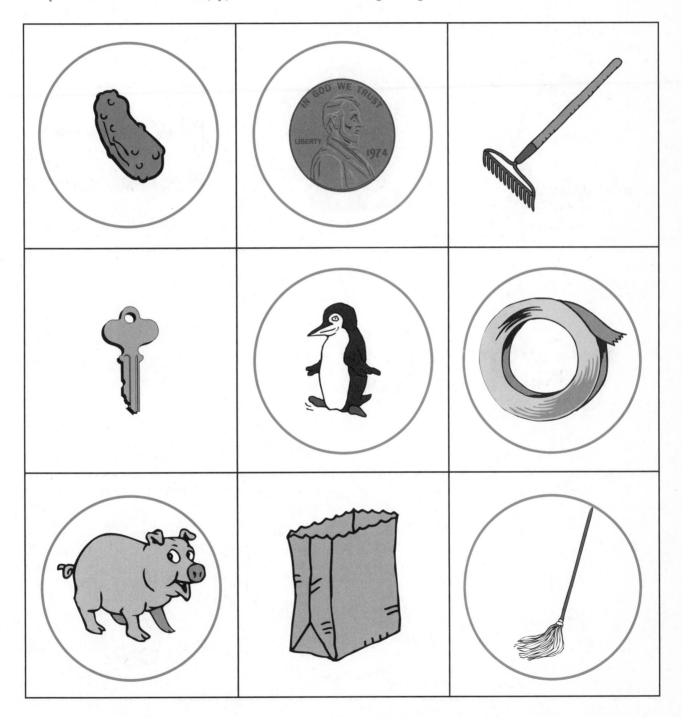

Name _____ **Date** _____

Name each picture. If students hear the /l/ sound in the picture name, they should circle the picture. Tell them that /l/ can come at the beginning or the end.

Name _____ **Date** _____

Name each picture. If students hear the /o/ sound in the picture name, they should circle the picture.

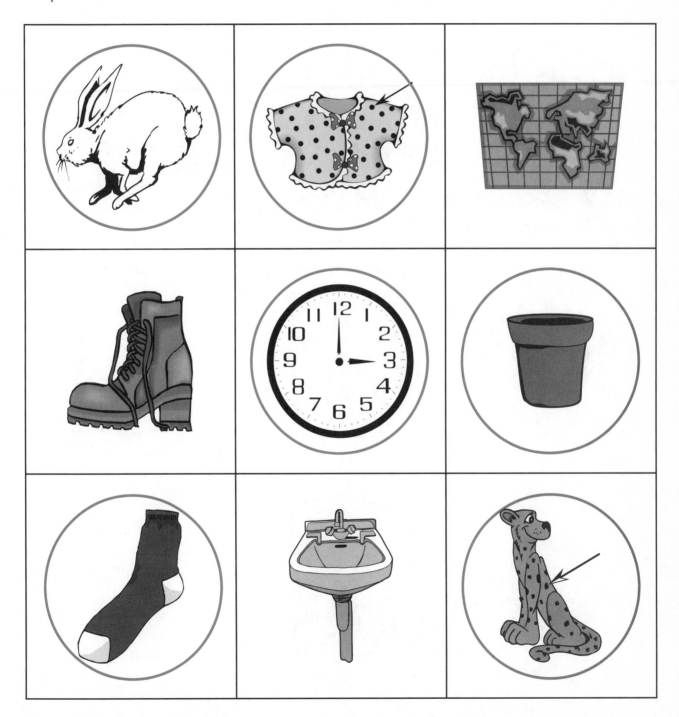

Name _____ Date _____

Name each picture. If students hear the /b/ sound in the picture name, they should circle the picture. Tell them that /b/ can come at the beginning or the end of the word.

Name _____ Date _____

Name each picture. Have students circle the letter that stands for the beginning sound in the word.

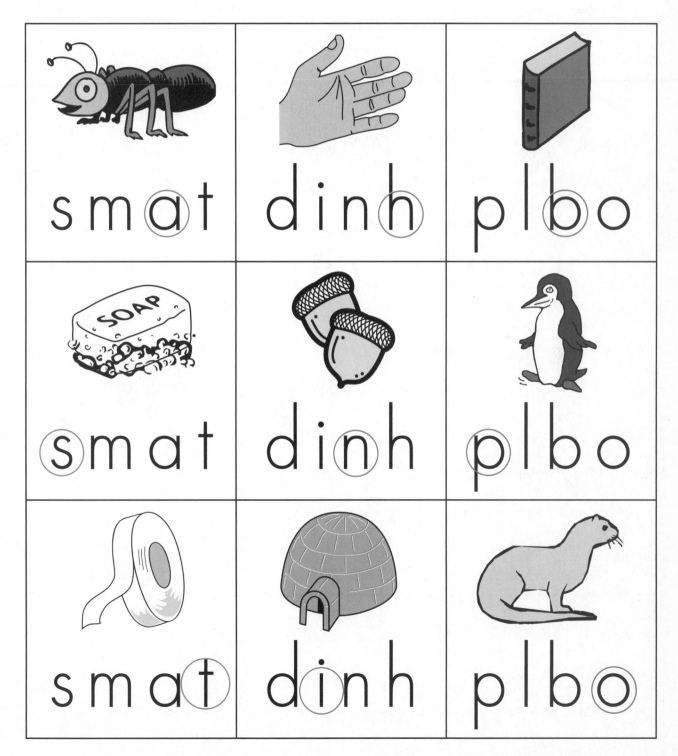

Name _____ **Date** _____

Name each picture. Then have students write the consonant letter that begins the word.

camel

can

cut

cat

cab

cot

Name _____ **Date** _____

Name each picture. Then have students write the missing consonant letters to complete the word.

| ma**s**k | mil**k** | **k**it |
| so**c**k | ta**c**k | **r**o**c**k |

Name _____ Date _____

Name each picture. Then have students write the missing consonant letter to complete the word.

rock

crab

ramp

drip

ram

drop

rip

rug

rib

Name _____ **Date** _____

Name each picture. Then have students write the missing consonant letter to complete the word.

fin

fan

floss

flock

raft

fast

Name _____ Date _____

Name each picture and help students hear each sound in the word. Have students find the word in the box that names the picture and write it under the picture.

| kiss | kick | crack | ram | rock | flat |

kick

rock

crack

flat

ram

kiss

Name _____ **Date** _____

Name each picture. Then have students write the consonant letter that completes the word.

frog

pig

gift

bag

dig

dog

Name _____ **Date** _____

Name each picture. Then have students write the missing consonant letters to complete the word.

j am

j et

j ump

j u dge

b ri dge

h e dge

Name _____ **Date** _____

Name each picture. Then have students write the missing vowel letter.

bug

cut

nuts

pup

mug

cuff

rug

drum

jug

Name _____ **Date** _____

Read each sentence with students. Then have students circle the capital letters in the sentence.

1. (K)atie lives near (O)cean (P)ark.

2. (H)er house is on (B)each (R)oad.

3. (S)he has a dog named (D)igger.

4. (H)e is part (L)ab and part (I)rish setter.

Have students identify each letter and then write the lower cases or capital letter that matches it.

E	e	Y	y	G	g	a	A
p	P	D	d	i	I	H	h
T	t	b	B	M	m	r	R

Name _____ **Date** _____

Name each picture and help students hear each sound in the word. Have students find the word in the box that names the picture and write it under the picture.

| jug | judge | buzz | fizz | gift | zero |

fizz   zero   buzz

jug   gift   judge

Name _____ **Date** _____

Name each picture. Then have students write the consonant letter that ends the word.

fox   six   ox

mix   box   fix

Name _____ **Date** _____

Name each picture. Then have students write the missing vowel letter.

n e t	b e d	w e t
l e g	p e t	j e t
p e n	h e n	b e g

Name _____ Date _____

Read each set of three words. Have students circle the two words in which *-ed* stands for the same sound.

1. helped   (started)   (landed)

2. (crossed)   (asked)   counted

3. lasted   (circled)   (called)

4. (locked)   (passed)   answered

5. (liked)   (missed)   trusted

6. (cared)   counted   (begged)

7. hoped   (landed)   (lasted)

8. spotted   (stopped)   (dropped)

9. (camped)   planned   (reached)

10. minded   (mixed)   (looked)

     Intervention

Name _____ **Date** _____

Name each picture. Then have students write the missing consonant letters to complete the word.

block   train   cloud

stick   glass   draw

UNIT 2 · Lesson 15

Name _____ **Date** _____

Name each picture. Then have students write the letters to finish the word that names the picture.

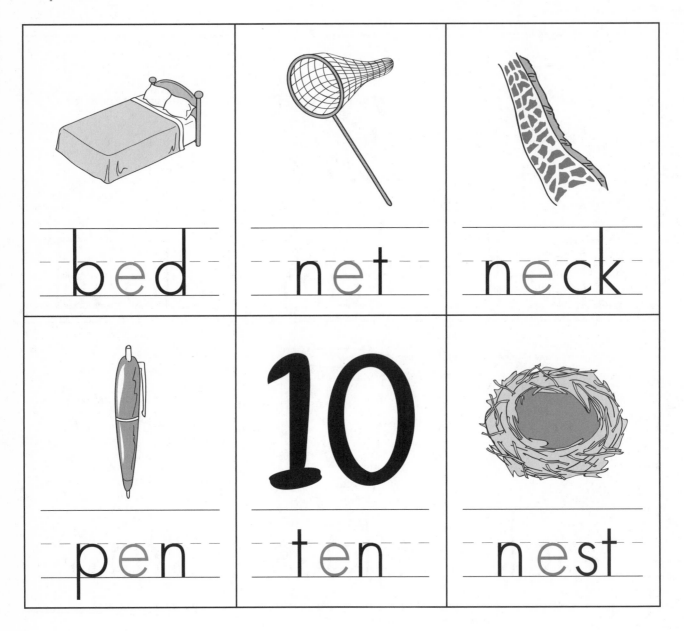

bed net neck

pen ten nest

Name _____ **Date** _____

Name each picture. If students hear the /sh/ sound at the beginning or the end of the word, tell them to write *sh* to complete the word. Have students read each word.

s<u>h</u>ip   s<u>h</u>ell   s<u>h</u>op

fi<u>sh</u>   bru<u>sh</u>   di<u>sh</u>

Name _____ **Date** _____

Name each picture. If students hear the /th/ sound at the beginning or the end of the word, tell them to write *th* to complete the word. Have students read each word.

cloth

path

math

thin

bath

moth

Name _____ **Date** _____

Name each picture. Ask if students hear /ch/ at the beginning or the end of the word. Then have them write *ch* to complete the word.

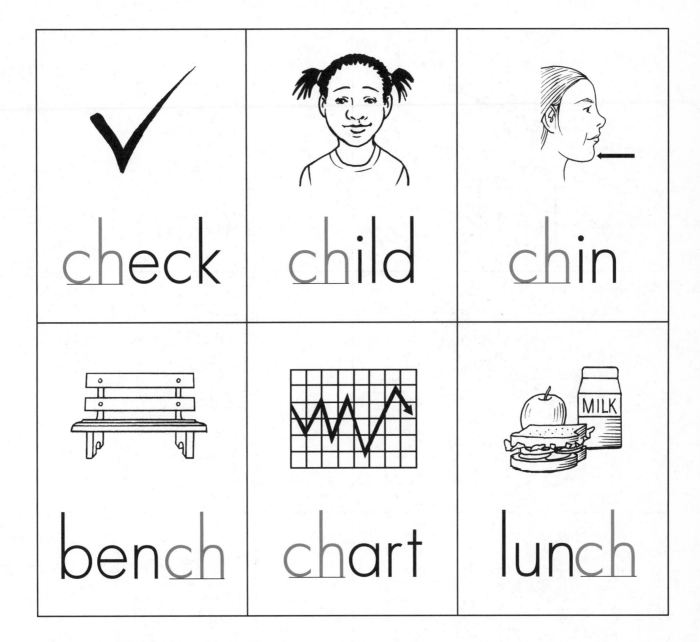

check

child

chin

bench

chart

lunch

Name _____ Date _____

Name each picture. Have students write *or* to complete each word.

f<u>or</u>k

h<u>or</u>n

c<u>or</u>n

st<u>or</u>m

sh<u>or</u>e

sc<u>or</u>e

Name _____ **Date** _____

Name each picture and help students hear each sound in the word. Have students find the word in the word box that names each picture and write it under the picture.

| path | catch | check | dish | store | horse |

check

dish

store

path

catch

horse

Name _____ **Date** _____

Name each picture. Then have the students write the letters to complete the word.

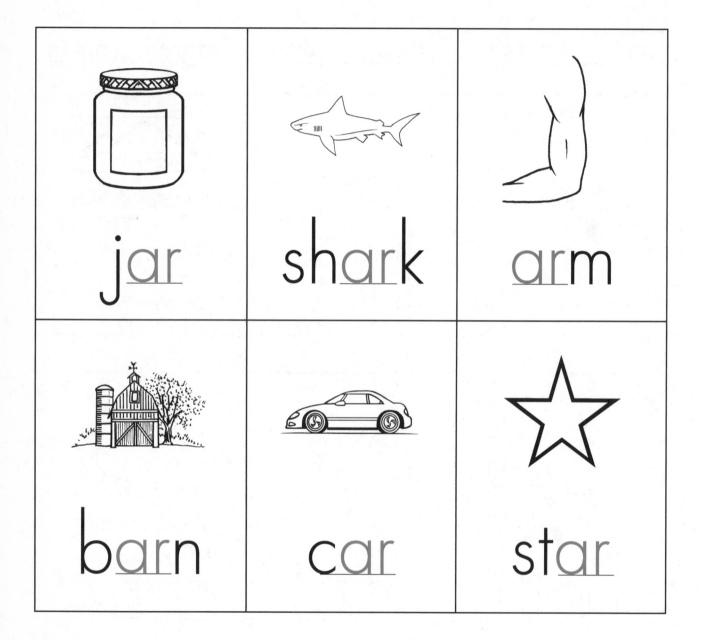

jar shark arm

barn car star

Name _____ **Date** _____

Read the words and identify the pictures. Have students write the word that matches each picture. Then have them circle the words that they wrote that end with silent *b*.

| lamb | crumbs | thumb | drums | plum | ram |

thumb

plum

ram

lamb

drums

crumbs

Name _____ **Date** _____

Read the words and identify the pictures. Have students write the word that matches each picture. Then have students circle the words that begin with *wh_*.

| walrus | wolf | wagon | what | wet | walnut |

wolf

wet

walrus

wagon

what

walnut

Name _____ **Date** _____

Read the words in the word box. Then name each picture. Have students match the word that names each picture with the word from the box it rhymes with and write it on the line.

curl	herd	hurt	turn	verb

1. herd

2. verb

3. turn

4. curl

5. hurt

Name _____ **Date** _____

Read each sentence. Have students add a period at the end if it is a telling sentence. Have students add a question mark if it is an asking sentence.

1. Where is the cat?

2. What did she do?

3. She hid in the basket.

4. What is her name?

5. It is Megan?

6. Megan is full of dust.

Name _____ **Date** _____

Name each picture. Then have the students write *ng* or *nk* to complete the word.

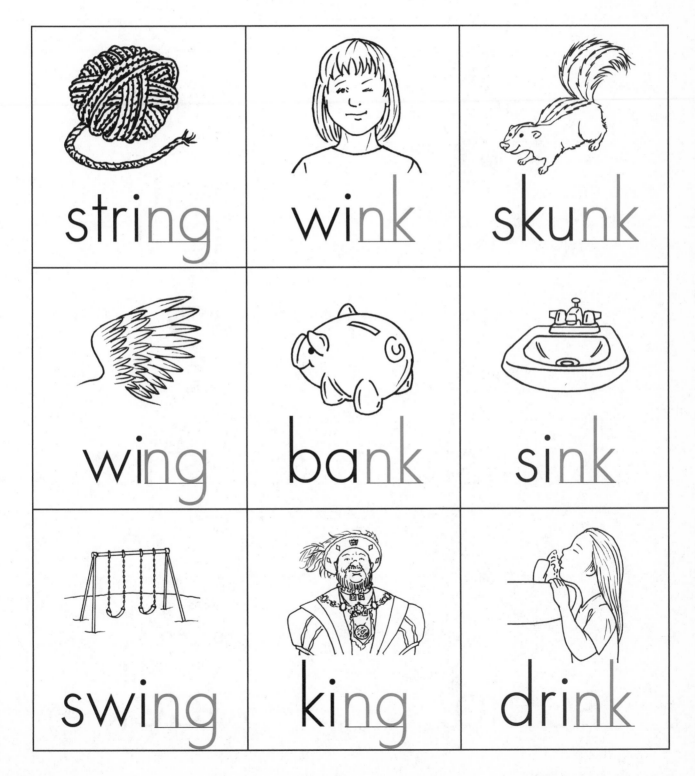

stri**ng**	wi**nk**	sku**nk**
wi**ng**	ba**nk**	si**nk**
swi**ng**	ki**ng**	dri**nk**

Name _____ **Date** _____

Name each picture. Then have students write the missing letters to complete the word.

qu<u>ee</u>n

qu<u>i</u>lt

s<u>qu</u>ish

<u>qu</u>estion

s<u>qu</u>id

<u>qu</u>ack

Name _____ **Date** _____

Name each picture. Then have students write the word that names the picture.

sink

wink

bank

wing

drink

ring

Name _____ Date _____

Name each picture. Ask if students hear /y/ or /v/ at the beginning of the word. Then have them write the missing letter to complete the word.

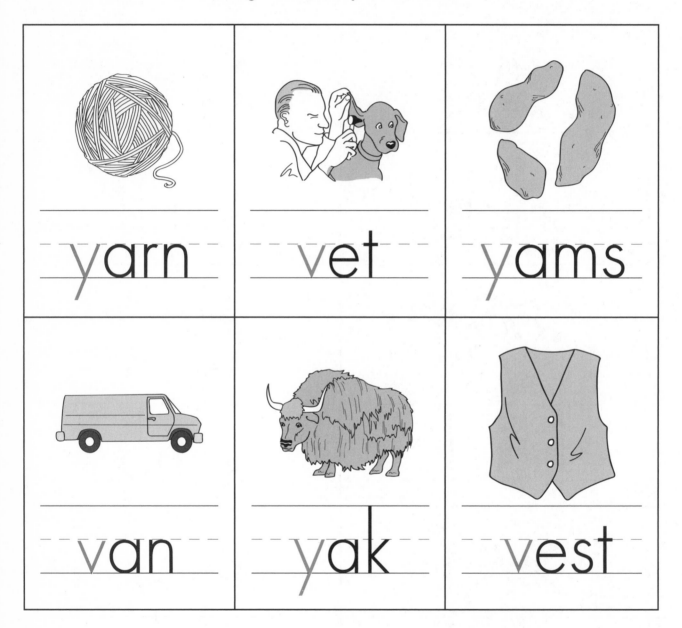

yarn

vet

yams

van

yak

vest

Name _____ Date _____

Name each picture. Have students add the syllable *-le* to the letters to complete the word. Then read the word together.

paddle

puzzle

squiggle

saddle

bubble

puddle

Name _____ **Date** _____

Name each picture. Then have students add the missing letters to complete each word.

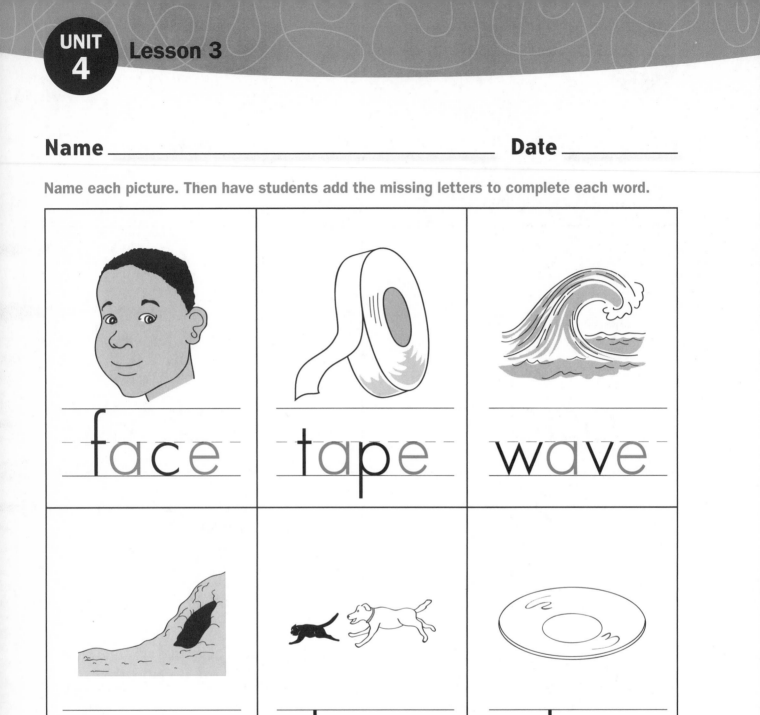

face

tape

wave

cave

chase

plate

Name _____ **Date** _____

Have students read the words in each line and circle the one that does not rhyme with the others.

1. snake   bake   shake   (black)

2. tame   name   (ham)   blame

3. skate   (street)   late   rate

4. (mad)   wade   fade   made

5. tape   (slap)   cape   shape

6. gave   save   (made)   brave

Name _____ **Date** _____

Read each sentence. Have students place a period or an exclamation point at the end of each one.

1. The street is very busy.

2. There are lots of cars and trucks.

3. Don't cross now!

4. It's not safe!

5. Stay here on the sidewalk.

6. Wait for the light to change.

7. Then we can cross.

8. Let's go!

Name _____ **Date** _____

Name each picture. Then have students add the missing letters to complete each word.

nine

smile

bride

tile

hive

drive

Name _____ Date _____

Read the words below. Each one names a familiar object. Have students decide which words name things found or used indoors and which name things found or used outdoors. Tell them to write them in the boxes.

rake	carpet	dishwasher	hose
oven	motorcycle	bookcase	sofa
shovel	umbrella	rowboat	bathtub

Indoors	Outdoors
carpet	rake
dishwasher	hose
oven	motorcycle
bookcase	shovel
sofa	umbrella
bathtub	rowboat

Name _____ Date _____

Name each picture. Then have students write the missing letters to complete each word.

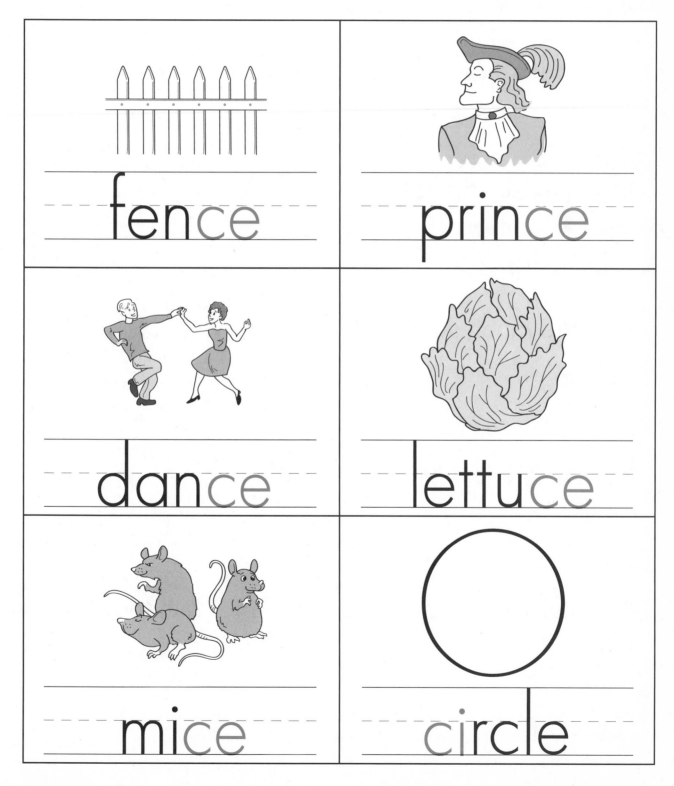

fence

prince

dance

lettuce

mice

circle

Name _____ Date _____

Read the words. Read the sentences. Have students write the word from the box that completes each sentence.

stage	cage	ginger	gentle

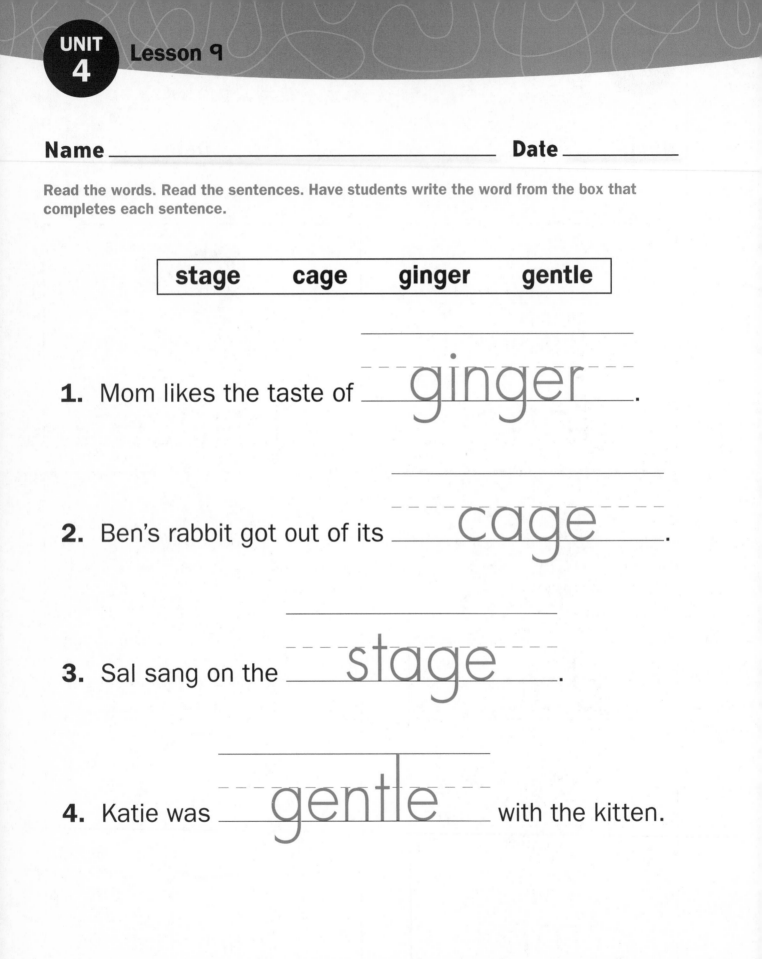

1. Mom likes the taste of ___ginger___.

2. Ben's rabbit got out of its ___cage___.

3. Sal sang on the ___stage___.

4. Katie was ___gentle___ with the kitten.

Name _____ **Date** _____

Remind students that imperative sentences give a command. Read the sentences to students. Have students circle the words that make the sentence a command.

1. Clay, (put your book) in your backpack.

2. Please (pass me) the jelly.

3. (Put the scarecrow) in the field.

4. You need to (ride your skateboard) carefully.

Name _____ Date _____

Name each picture. Have students write the missing letters to complete each word.

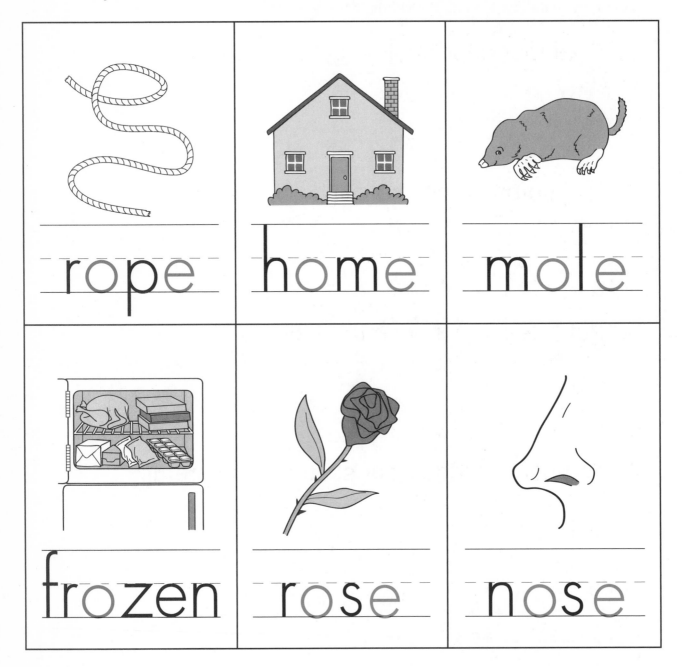

rope   home   mole

frozen   rose   nose

Intervention

Name _____ **Date** _____

Have students write -er or –est to the given word to spell words that tell about each picture.

1.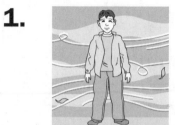

                                     cold

2.

    colder

3.

coldest

Name _____ **Date** _____

Read the words below. Have students write each word below the picture it names.

computer	cube	cucumber
mule	music	pupil

music

cucumber

cube

mule

computer

pupil

Name _____ **Date** _____

Have students add the letters given to the beginning of each sound to complete the word. Tell students to write two words that rhyme.

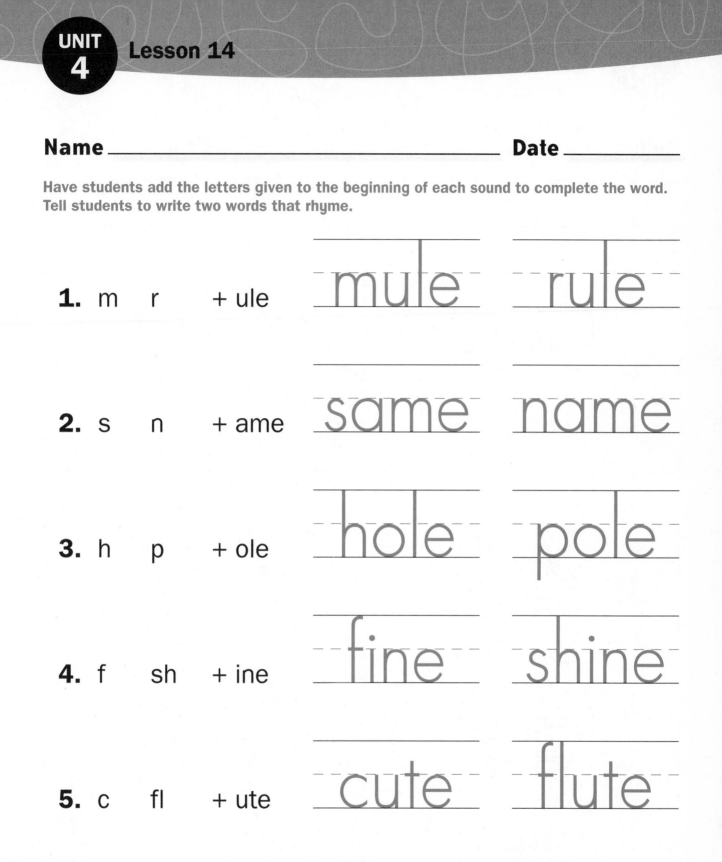

1. m   r   + ule   mule   rule

2. s   n   + ame   same   name

3. h   p   + ole   hole   pole

4. f   sh   + ine   fine   shine

5. c   fl   + ute   cute   flute

6. h   m   + ope   hope   mope

Name _____ **Date** _____

Name each picture. Then have the students write the word that names the picture.

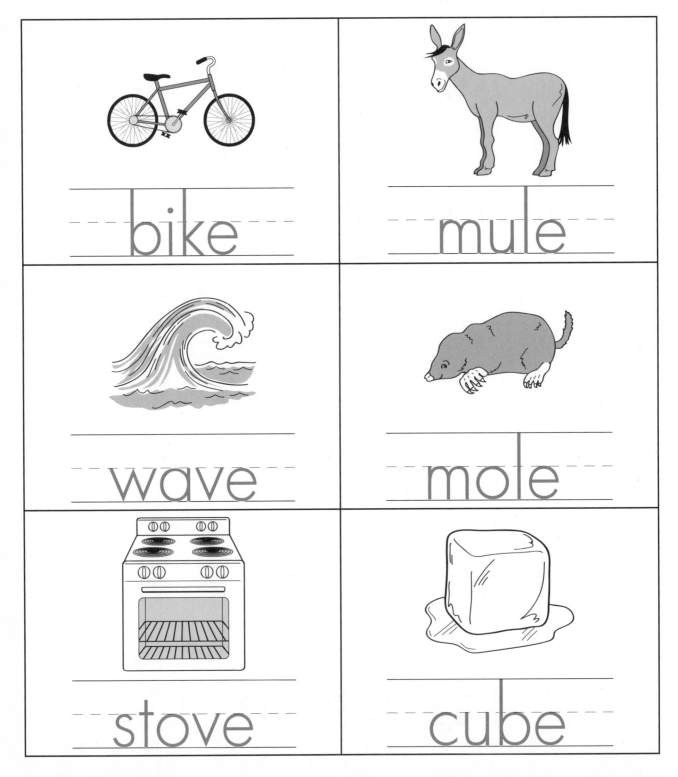

bike

mule

wave

mole

stove

cube

Intervention

Lesson 1

Name ______________________ **Date** __________

Read the following words to students. Tell students to circle the words that have the /ē/ sound.

Steve	hide
learn	she
complete	tie
me	athlete
ate	create
he	move

Name _____ **Date** _____

Read the sentences. Have students rewrite them using capital letters where they belong.

1. lena has a dog named pete.

2. steve likes to swim on saturdays.

3. Beth and i will go to indiana.

Intervention

Name _____ **Date** _____

Part 1

Name each picture. Then have students add *ee* to complete the picture words.

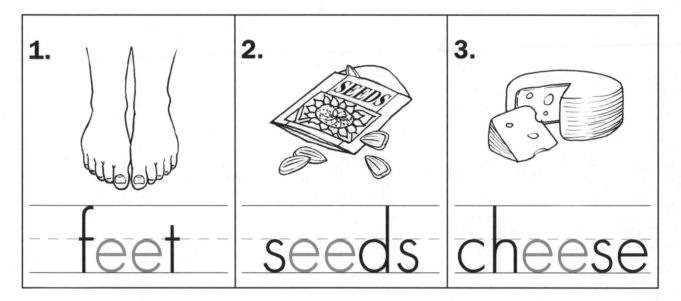

1. feet
2. seeds
3. cheese

Part 2

Name each picture. Then have students add *ea* to complete the picture words.

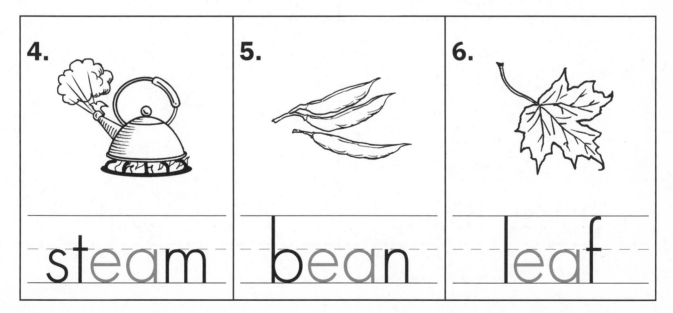

4. steam
5. bean
6. leaf

Name _____ **Date** _____

Name the pictures. Have students circle the word that matches the picture.

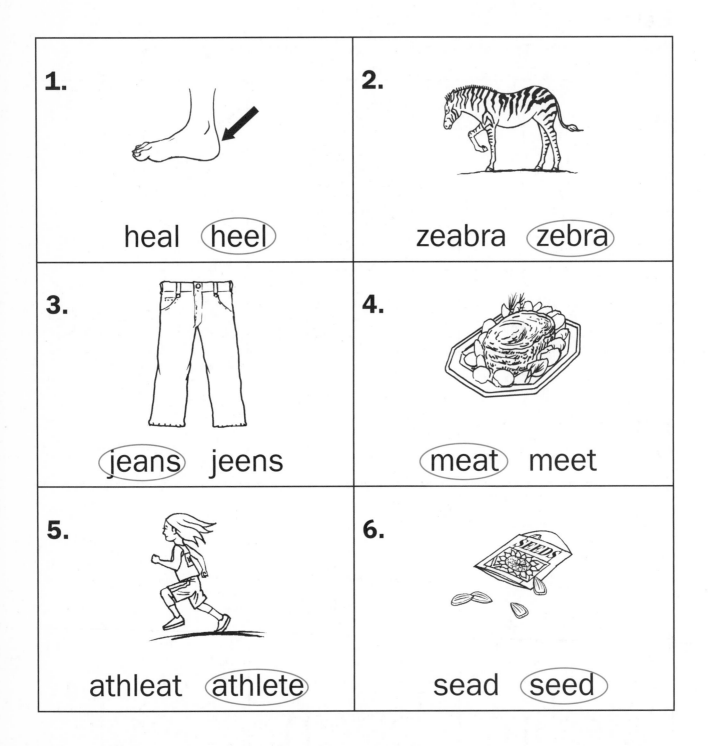

1. heal (heel)

2. zeabra (zebra)

3. (jeans) jeens

4. (meat) meet

5. athleat (athlete)

6. sead (seed)

Name _____ **Date** _____

Read the words. Have students circle the words that have the /ē/ sound. Have students reread all words they circled.

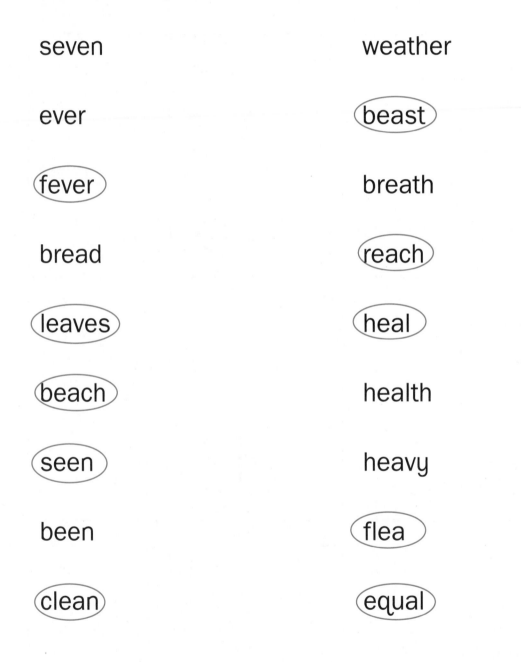

seven

ever

(fever)

bread

(leaves)

(beach)

(seen)

been

(clean)

weather

(beast)

breath

(reach)

(heal)

health

heavy

(flea)

(equal)

Name _____ Date _____

Add _y_ to write a word that describes the weather in each picture.

1. windy

2. rainy

3. snowy

4. cloudy

5. misty

6. stormy

Intervention

Name _____ **Date** _____

Have students rewrite each sentence, using correct capitalization and punctuation whenever they are needed.

1. spring begins in march

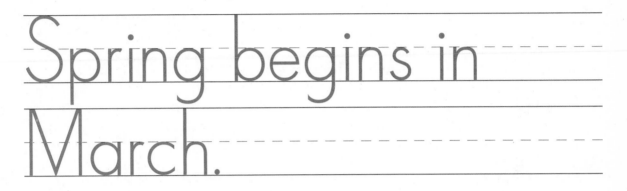

Spring begins in March.

2. summer begins in june

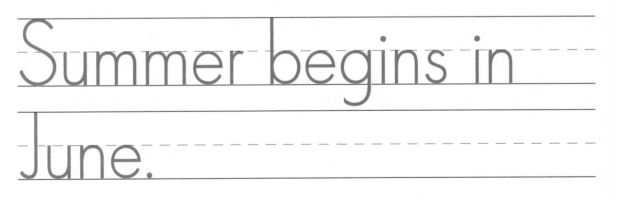

Summer begins in June.

3. fall begins in september

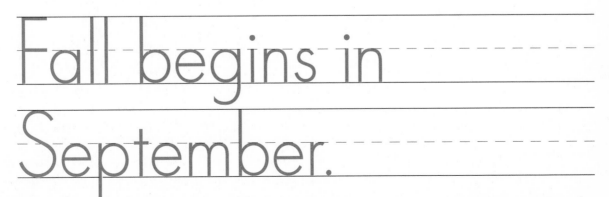

Fall begins in September.

Name _____ Date _____

Read each sentence and the words in the box. Tell students to choose a word from the box and write it on the line.

| icy | spicy | lacy | fancy |

1.

Tracy has a _____lacy_____ shirt.

2.

Marcy eats _____spicy_____ things.

3.

The lake is _____icy_____.

4.

Sally has a _____fancy_____ bike.

Name _____ **Date** _____

Have students re-write the day, month, or date correctly on the line.

1. thursday

2. april

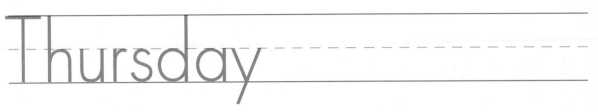

3. february 9 2006

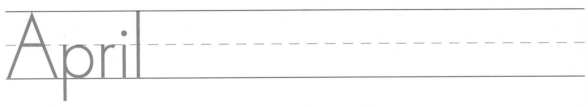

4. october

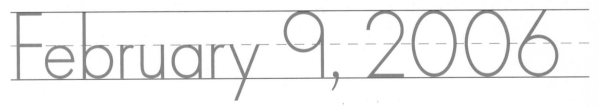

5. monday

Name _____ **Date** _____

Read the words. Then read the sentences. Have students write the word to complete each sentence.

| reads | field | sunny | busy | fancy | green |

1. Sunglasses are for _____sunny_____ days.

2. Annie is _____busy_____ with her work.

3. Every horse had a _____fancy_____ ribbon.

4. Eve _____reads_____ many books.

5. Tracy eats _____green_____ peas.

6. Danny runs in a grassy _____field_____ .

Name _____ Date _____

Name the pictures. Then have students complete the words by adding *ai* or *ay*.

1. snail

2. play

3. clay

4. train

5. paint

6. tray

Name _____ **Date** _____

Name each picture. Have students write the plural form of the words in the box to name each picture. Circle the words where you changed *y* to *i* and added *es*.

bird	frog	puppy	bug	desk	bunny

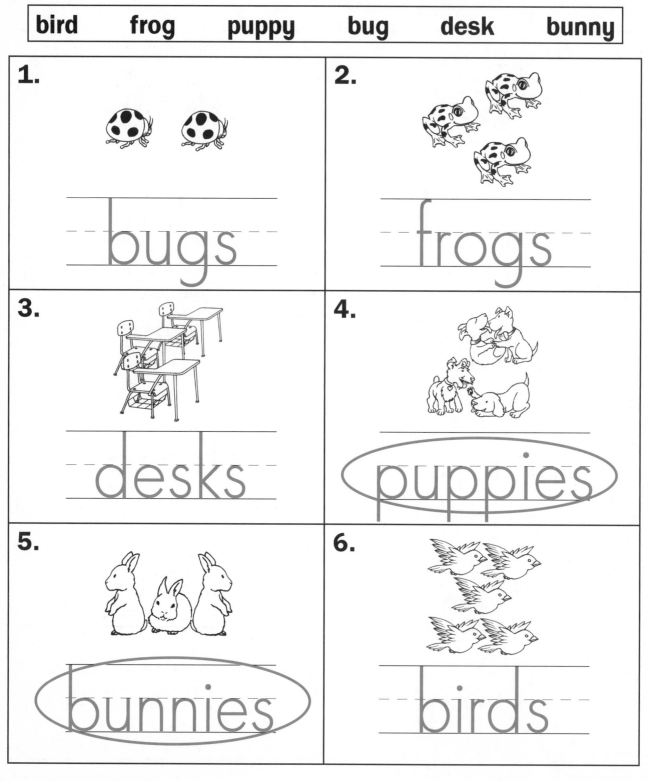

1. bugs

2. frogs

3. desks

4. (puppies)

5. (bunnies)

6. birds

Name _____ Date _____

Name the pictures. Have students add *i_e*, *–igh*, *-ie*, or *-y* to complete each word.

1. drive

2. night

3. dry

4. tie

5. light

6. cry

Name _____ **Date** _____

Have students write a rhyming word to complete each sentence.

1. When the moon is bright, the night is full of

light .

2. Daddy spilled some pie on his brand-new

tie .

3. A bird can fly way up in the ___ sky ___.

4. We did not wash my jeans right, and now they're

much too tight .

Name _____ **Date** _____

Name each picture. Then have the students write the letters that spell the vowel sound in each word.

| ay | y | ai | ea | igh | ee |

1. bright

2. clay

3. mail

4. fry

5. street

6. jeans

Name _____ Date _____

Name each picture. Have students add *oa* or *ow* to complete the word that names each picture.

1.

coat

2.

elbow

3.

goat

4.

toast

5.

snow

6.

boat

Name _____ **Date** _____

Have students rewrite each sentence, using capital letters and punctuation where they are needed.

1. grandma lives in tampa florida.

Grandma lives in Tampa, Florida.

2. sarah visited cape may new jersey.

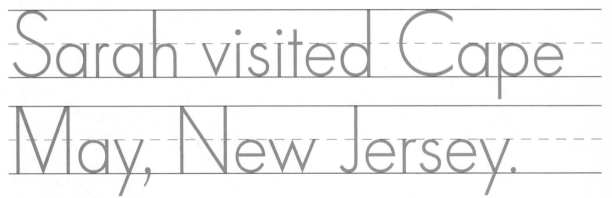

Sarah visited Cape May, New Jersey.

3. dad grew up in detroit michigan.

Dad grew up in Detroit, Michigan.

Name _____ Date _____

Read the sentences. Have students write *ew* or *ue* to complete the word in each sentence.

1. Jan has a n__ew__ dress.

2. Huey came to the resc__ue__ of the lady who fell.

3. Katie val__ue__s a good book.

4. There are a f__ew__ dogs I like.

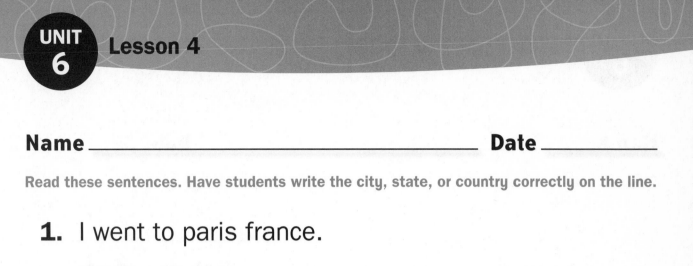

Name _____ **Date** _____

Read these sentences. Have students write the city, state, or country correctly on the line.

1. I went to paris france.

Paris, France

2. The plane few into dallas texas.

Dallas, Texas

3. Kato was born in tokyo japan.

Tokyo, Japan

4. She will go to frankfurt germany and london england on her trip.

Frankfurt, Germany London, England

Name _____ **Date** _____

Read the words and sentences. Then have students use the words to complete the sentences.

continue	few	follow	Oak	road

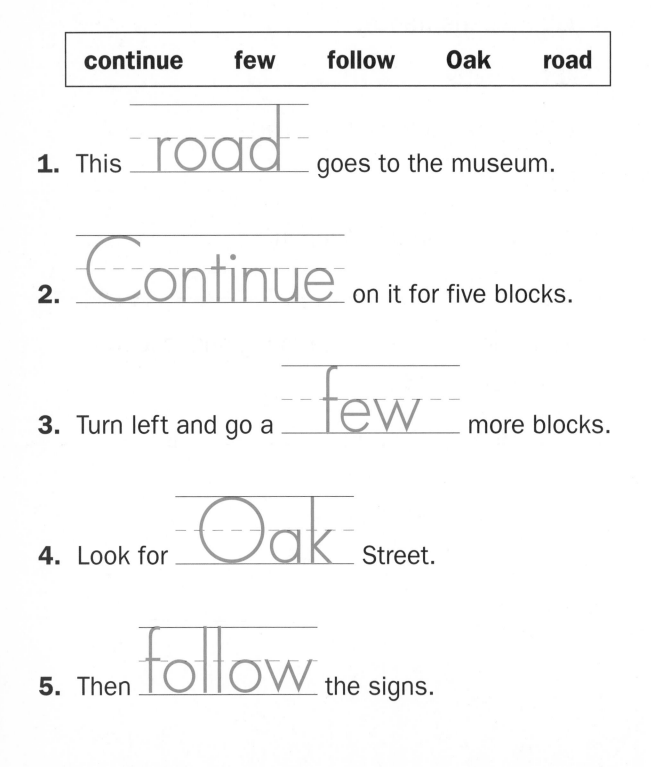

1. This ___road___ goes to the museum.

2. ___Continue___ on it for five blocks.

3. Turn left and go a ___few___ more blocks.

4. Look for ___Oak___ Street.

5. Then ___follow___ the signs.

Name _____ Date _____

Name the pictures. Then have students write *oo* to complete the picture word.

1.

goose

2.

boot

3.

moon

4.

spoon

5.

tooth

6.

roof

Name _____ **Date** _____

Read each pair of words with the students. Have them circle the word in each pair that has the sound /o͞o/.

1. (food)   foot

2. carton   (cartoon)

3. puddle   (poodle)

4. (stool)   stood

5. took   (tool)

6. (cocoon)   cocoa

7. cook   (cool)

8. (mood)   wood

Name _____ **Date** _____

Name each picture. Then have students complete the word that names each picture by adding *u_e*, *ue*, or *u*.

1. tuba

2. tulip

3. ruler

4. glue

5. clue

6. tuna

Name _____ **Date** _____

Have students rewrite each sentence, using capital letters where they are needed. Then read the sentences together and have students circle the words they wrote that have the /o͞o/ sound.

1. tuesday is sue's birthday.

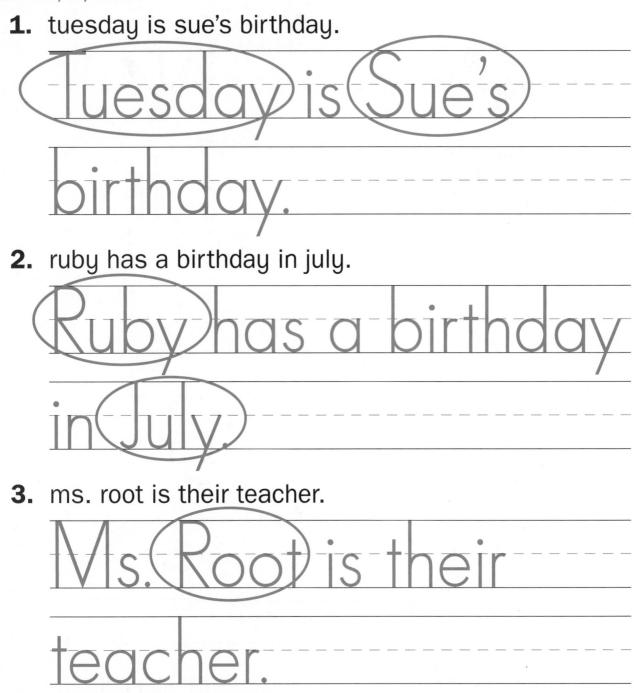

Tuesday is Sue's birthday.

2. ruby has a birthday in july.

Ruby has a birthday in July.

3. ms. root is their teacher.

Ms. Root is their teacher.

Name _____ **Date** _____

Read each pair of sentences with the students. Then have them combine the two sentences to write one sentence.

1. The zoo has a fox. The zoo has a yak.

The zoo has a fox and a yak.

2. Sue needs string. Sue needs glue.

Sue needs string and glue.

3. Max is tired. Max is hungry.

Max is tired and hungry.

Name _____ **Date** _____

Read each sentence and the words below the sentence. Have students circle the word that correctly completes the sentence and write it on the line.

1. Rue has a ___blue___ bike.

   (blue) blew

2. Drew ___chews___ his food.

   choose (chews)

3. This library book is ___due___ tomorrow.

   (due) dew

4. Ms. Adams ___flew___ to Dallas.

   flu (flew)

Name _____ Date _____

Read the sentences together. Have students number them from 1 to 5 to show the order in which they probably happened.

5   They took the bus home.

3   They walked to the museum.

2   She met Stuart at school.

4   Stuart saw the dinosaurs.

1   Mom left work early.

Name _____ Date _____

Name the pictures. Have students write the word with the /oo/ sound that names each picture.

| cook | hook | wood | book | hood | brook |

1.

book

2.

wood

3.

hood

4.

cook

5.

hook

6.

brook

Name _____ **Date** _____

Read each sentence. Have students write the word from the word box that correctly completes the sentence.

wood	look	cook	book	hood

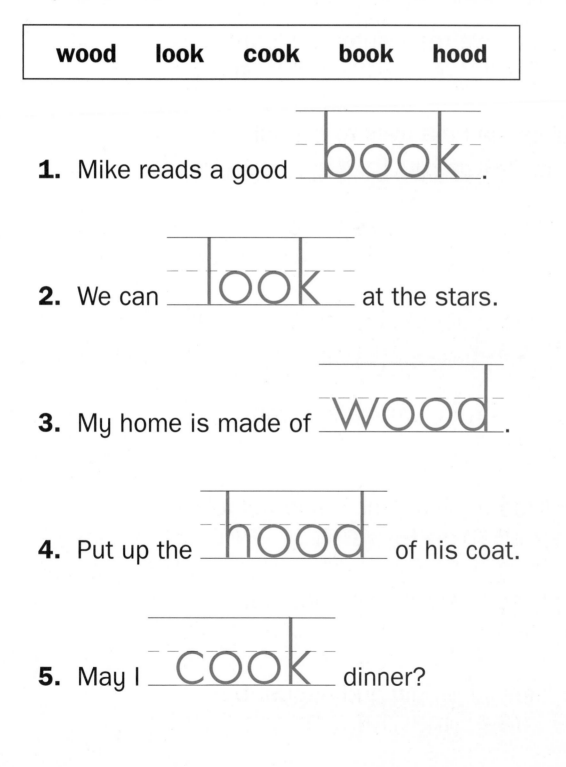

1. Mike reads a good ___book___.

2. We can ___look___ at the stars.

3. My home is made of ___wood___.

4. Put up the ___hood___ of his coat.

5. May I ___cook___ dinner?

Name _____ Date _____

Read each sentence, pausing briefly where commas belong. Have students add the commas. Then read the sentence again together.

1. In school, we read write and learn.
In school, we read, write, and learn.

2. Amy Hal and Pia walk to school.
Amy, Hal, and Pia walk to school.

3. Max Kayla and Jo take the bus.
Max, Kayla, and Jo take the bus.

4. I like books about dogs cats and kids.
I like books about dogs, cats, and kids.

5. Pia likes to run jump and climb.
Pia likes to run, jump, and climb.

6. Max likes to sing dance and tell jokes.
Max likes to sing, dance, and tell jokes.

7. Amy likes to swim dive and float.
Amy likes to swim, dive ,and float.

8. She likes June July and August best.
She likes June, July, and August best.

Name _____ **Date** _____

Read the words with students. Have them circle the words where *ow* makes the /ow/ sound.

cow   tower

grow   power

how   shower

now   slower

snow   towel

show   growl

town   howl

down   showed

clown   crowd

grown   crowed

shown   mower

Name _____ **Date** _____

Read the words with students. Have them circle the words where *ou* makes the /ow/ sound.

(ouch)   tough

touch   (hour)

(pouch)   (house)

soup   (hound)

group   pour

(cloud)   (proud)

could   (mouse)

(count)   (mouth)

(scout)   your

(shout)   rough

should   (round)

Intervention

Name _____ **Date** _____

Read each word pair. Have students circle the word that has the /ow/ sound.

1. from　　　　　(frown)

2. (sound)　　　　sun

3. done　　　　　(down)

4. month　　　　(mouth)

Name _____ Date _____

Read the story.

Rosie Caught a Fish

"Dad, I want to learn how to fish!"

They sat by the lake.

Dad taught his daughter how to fish.

They wanted to be fishing by early morning.

Dad taught Rosie to cast the line and reel it in.

Rosie wanted a fish, so she waited and waited.

She thought she might never catch a fish.

Rosie felt a tug on her line.

She brought it in slowly like she was taught.

"Dad, I caught a fish!"

Draw a picture of the characters from the story.

Ask students the first question before they complete the story. Then have them answer the remaining questions. When possible, have students answer by pointing to and reading aloud the answers in the text.

• Based on the title, what do you think might happen in the story? Possible Answer: *I think Rosie will catch a really big fish.*

• Who taught Rosie how to fish? *Rosie's dad taught her to fish.*

• How many fish did Rosie catch? *Rosie caught one fish.*

Name _____ **Date** _____

Read the sentences. Have students add quotation marks where they belong.

1. Let's play a game, said Lia.

"Let's play a game," said Lia.

2. What game? asked Robbie.

"What game?" asked Robbie.

3. What about jacks? said Emma.

"What about jacks?" said Emma.

4. I like Go Fish, said Lia.

"I like Go Fish," said Lia.

5. I'll play Go Fish, said Robbie.

"I'll play Go Fish," said Robbie.

6. Do you have cards? asked Emma.

"Do you have cards?" asked Emma.

7. I'll ask Mom for some, said Lia.

"I'll ask Mom for some," said Lia.

8. OK. Let's play! said Emma.

"OK. Let's play!" said Emma.

Name _____ Date _____

Read the words and sentences. Complete the sentence by writing the correct word on the line.

know   **no**
_____

1. There are ___no___ kids at the park.

2. I don't ___know___ where they are.

knew   **new**
_____

3. My brother got a ___new___ bike.

4. I ___knew___ he was getting one.

night   **knight**

5. We watched a movie last ___night___.

6. It was about a kind ___knight___ and a king.

Name _____ Date _____

Name the pictures. Write *aw* to complete the picture word.

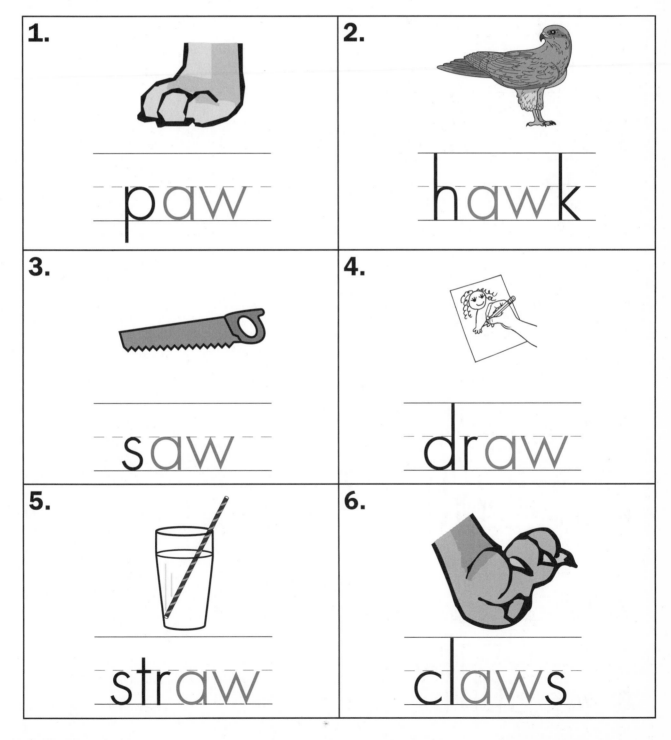

1. paw	**2.** hawk
3. saw	**4.** draw
5. straw	**6.** claws

Name _____ **Date** _____

Say each word, adding the /aw/ sound where the missing letters are. Then have students add *all* to complete the word.

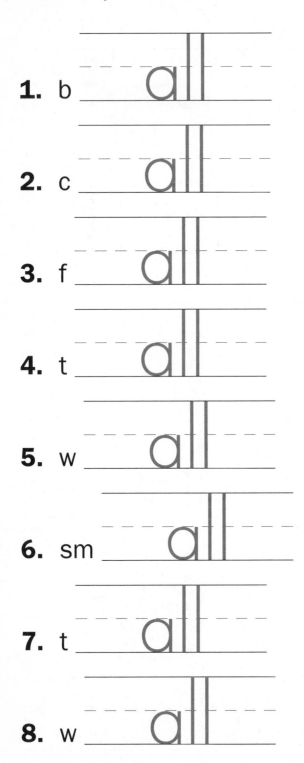

1. b _____ a l l

2. c _____ a l l

3. f _____ a l l

4. t _____ a l l

5. w _____ a l l

6. sm _____ a l l

7. t _____ a l l

8. w _____ a l l

Name _____ **Date** _____

Read the words in the box. Write the word on the line to complete each sentence.

bought	caught	taught	thought

1. I ___caught___ the ball.

2. You ___taught___ Willy to ride a bike.

3. Mom ___bought___ apples, milk, and beans at the store.

4. I ___thought___ the book was really funny.

Name _____ Date _____

Read the story.

A Flat!

Mitch lifted boxes of fruit.

He filled his red truck.

Mitch looked at his tire.

"It is flat!" he said. "Can I fix it?" Mitch asked.

If Mitch gets patches, he can.

Mitch worked hard to fix his truck tire.

Look at its patches!

The red patches match his red truck!

Illustrate an event from the story.

After students have read the story, ask them the following questions. When possible, have students answer by pointing to and reading aloud the answers in the text.

- What question appears in the selection? Can the question be answered? *The question in the selection is* Can I fix it? *The question is answered—Mitch fixes the tire.*
- What is inside the boxes Mitch loads into his truck? Possible Answer: *Mitch loads fruit into his truck.*
- How does Mitch fix his tire? *Mitch uses patches to fix his tire.*

Name _____ **Date** _____

Read the words with students. Have them circle the words that have the /aw/ sound.

(bought)   shall

rough   (small)

(cough)   (call)

(brought)   calf

(thought)   (hall)

tough   (halt)

(caught)   half

(taught)   (haul)

laugh   (walk)

(daughter)   (talk)

Name _____ Date _____

Read each sentence. Rewrite the sentence replacing the underlined word or words with a pronoun.

1. <u>Franny</u> bought a book.

She bought a book.

2. She brought <u>the book</u> to school.

She brought it to school.

3. <u>Mae and I</u> want to read the book.

We want to read the book.

Name _____ Date _____

Name the pictures. Write *oy* or *oi* to complete each picture word.

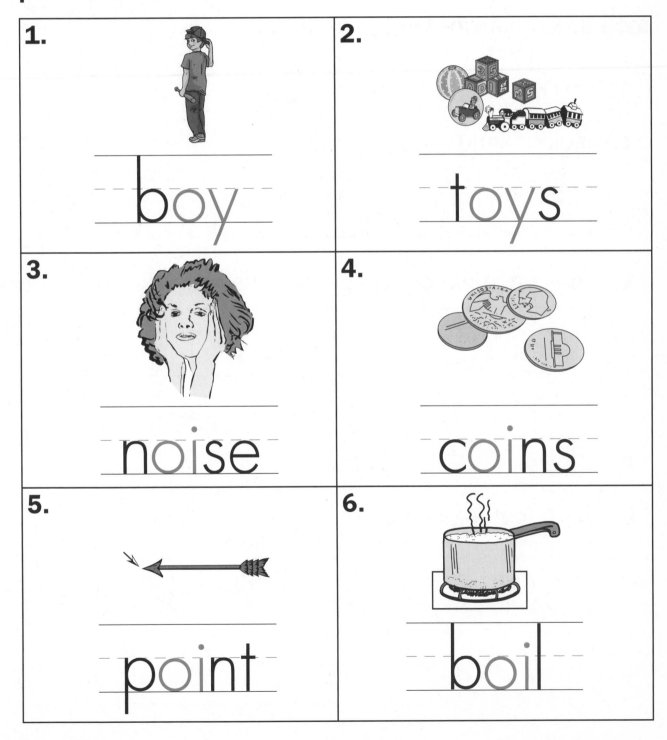

1. boy

2. toys

3. noise

4. coins

5. point

6. boil

Name _____ **Date** _____

Read each sentence. Rewrite the sentence, replacing the possessive noun with a possessive pronoun. You may use each word only one time.

| his | its | her | your | my |

1. <u>Jack's</u> friends have pets.

His friends have pets.

2. I call each pet by <u>the pet's</u> name.

I call each pet by
its name.

3. <u>Ellie's</u> cat is named Ed.

Her cat is named Ed.

Name _____ Date _____

Name each picture. Write *r* or *wr* to complete the word under the picture.

1.

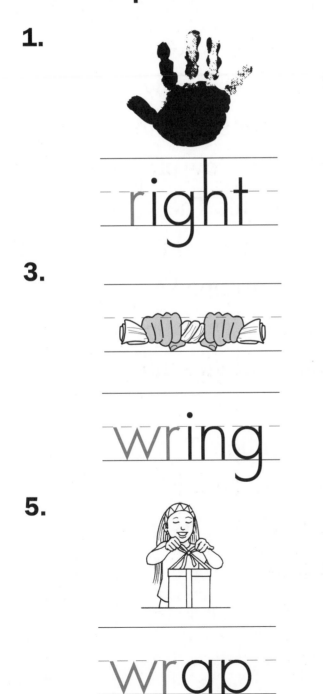

right

2.

write

3.

wring

4.

ring

5.

wrap

Name _____ **Date** _____

Read the story.

The Clever Crow

A crow flew a long way. It needed water. It had not rained. Water was scarce. The crow knew it must find water soon. Then it saw some water in a large crack in a rock. The crow put its beak into the crack. It tried to drink. The crow's beak was too big to get into the crack.

Then the crow had an idea. It dropped a small stone into the crack. The crow saw the water rise a little. It kept dropping stones into the crack.

Finally the water was high enough. The crow took a long drink. It felt much better.

This trick had saved the crow's life.

Illustrate an event from the story.

After students have read the story, ask them the following questions. When possible, have students answer by pointing to and reading aloud the answers in the text.

- **What is this story about?** Possible Answer: *This story is about a thirsty crow.*
- **Why was the crow thirsty?** *It was thirsty because it had flown a long way.*
- **Why does the crow drop small stones into the crack?** *The crow drops small stones into the crack to make the water rise.*

Name _____ Date _____

Name each picture. Write *ph* to complete the picture names.

1. phone

2. photo

3. gopher

4. graph

5. elephant

6. dolphin

Name _____ Date _____

Read the sentences. Write the word from the box that correctly completes each sentence.

| phone | toy | boils | wraps | oil | photos |

1. Dad put _____oil_____ in the car.

2. The _____phone_____ rang at 10 p.m.

3. Janice _____wraps_____ the baby in a blanket.

4. Peter likes the _____toy_____ he got at the circus.

5. Mom _____boils_____ the pasta in a big pot.

6. Kristy put the _____photos_____ in frames.

Name _____ Date _____

Read the words with students. Have them circle the words that have the /er/ sound.

bear

beard

dear

(early)

(earth)

(earnest)

fear

gear

hear

(heard)

(learn)

near

pear

rear

tear

wear

year

(yearn)

Name _____ Date _____

Name each picture. Write *ey* to complete the picture names.

1. money

2. turkey

3. chimney

4. donkey

5. monkey

6. honey

Name _____ **Date** _____

Read each sentence. Rewrite the sentence, making it longer by using words that describe.

1. I have a cat. Possible answers:

I have a fluffy black and white cat.

2. The flowers are nice.

The red and pink flowers smell pretty.

3. We won the game.

We won the football game by seven points.

Name _____ **Date** _____

Read the story.

Cat Skates

Cat puts on his skates.

"You cannot skate," says Sheep.

"I can!" says Cat. "Here I go!"

The wheels spin. Cat goes fast. He skids and slips and slides. He skates onto the grass. He hits some stones. He trips and slams into a tree.

Crash! Down he goes!

Cat says, "See? I CAN skate!"

Sheep says, "Bah! You hit a tree!"

Cat says, "Ha! That is how I stop!"

Draw your favorite character from the story.

Ask students the first question before they complete the story. Then have them answer the remaining questions. When possible, have students answer by pointing to and reading aloud the answers in the text.

• Based on the title and the first two lines of the story, what do you predict will happen to Cat? Possible Answer: *I predict Cat will skate.*

• What happens when the wheels on Cat's skates first begin to spin? *Cat goes fast when his wheels start to spin.*

• In the end, does Cat skate? Possible Answer: *In the end, Cat skates, but he is not very good yet.*

Intervention

Name _____ Date _____

Read these words with students. Tell students that each word is missing a letter. Have them add the letter and write the word correctly.

1. erth   _earth_

2. mony   _money_

3. serch   _search_

4. turky   _turkey_

5. lern   _learn_

6. hony   _honey_

7. erly   _early_

8. monky   _monkey_

Name _____   Date _____

Read the sentences and the words under them. Circle the word that correctly completes each sentence and write it on the line.

1. The puppy wagged its ___tail___.

   (tail)   tale

2. This is our town's ___main___ street.

   (main)   mane

3. The boat has a red ___sail___.

   (sail)   sale

4. There are raindrops on the window ___pane___.

   pain   (pane)

5. The sick child looked ___pale___.

   pail   (pale)

Name _____ Date _____

Name each picture. Write the missing letters to complete the word.

snail

snake

train

frame

grapes

tail

Name _____ Date _____

Read each sentence. Write a question that the sentence above it would answer.

1. Bibi's house is in the next block.

   Possible Answer: Where is Bibi's house?

2. Nate got here at 4 o'clock.

   Possible Answer: When did Nate get here?

3. Julie walks to school.

   Possible Answer: How does Julie get to school?

4. Our team won the game.

   Possible Answer: Why did you celebrate?

5. Ellie bought a new pencil.

   Possible Answer: What did Ellie buy?

Name _____ Date _____

Read the story.

Nuts!

Look!

That big shell has nuts.

I shall crack that shell with my beak.

This shell is thick.

I shall smash it!

Smash it!

Crush it!

Crash it!

That big shell did not crack!

I shall call another bird for help.

I shall get nuts!

Illustrate an event from the story.

After students have read the story, ask them the following questions. When possible, have students answer by pointing to and reading aloud the answers in the text.

- **What is this story about? Possible Answer:** *This story is about a bird that has a hard time getting a nut out of a shell.*
- **What did the main character do to try to get the nuts out of the shell?** *The main character smashed, crushed, and crashed the shell to try to get the nuts.*
- **Who did the main character call to finally get some nuts?** *The main character called another bird to get some nuts.*

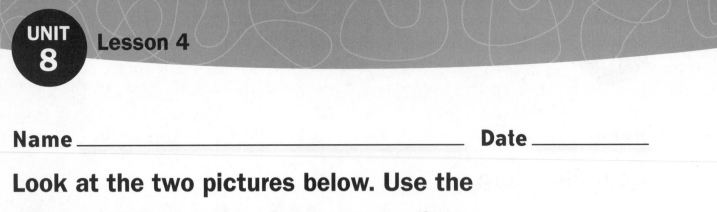
Name _____ Date _____

Look at the two pictures below. Use the chart to tell how the pictures are alike and how they are different.

TREE A

TREE B

TREE A	TREES A & B	TREE B
Possible Answers: short apple tree five branches round shape	Possible Answers: They both have leaves. They are both trees.	Possible Answers: tall oak tree bird's nest hole in trunk

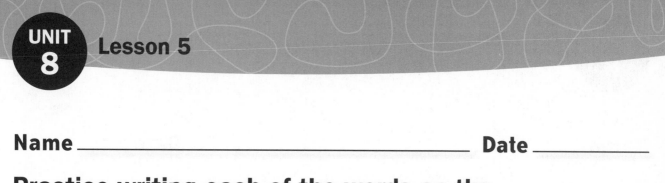

Name _____ Date _____

Practice writing each of the words on the lines. Then, rewrite the sentence making sure you form the letters correctly.

1. Annie   Annie

2. East   East

Lance moved to Newton, Indiana, from Florida.

Lance moved to Newton, Indiana, from Florida.

Check to make sure students have correctly formed all the letters, with an emphasis on capital letters A, N, E, F, I, and L.

Name _____ Date _____

Read each group of words. Circle the word that has the short i sound.

1. dry   (bit)   site

2. (him)   fox   my

3. pie   time   (sick)

4. (big)   hide   tug

5. lime   (pick)   might

6. wet   ride   (spill)

Name _____ Date _____

Name each picture. Write the missing letters to complete the word.

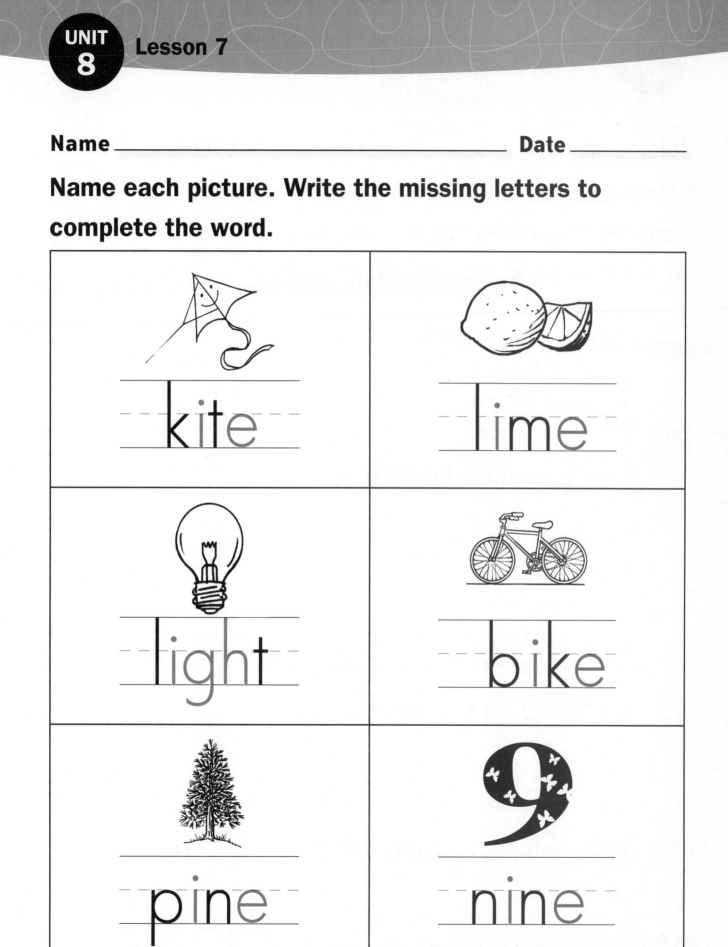

kite

lime

light

bike

pine

nine

Name _____ Date _____

Read these sentences. Then, rewrite each sentence by replacing the underlined word or words with a possessive pronoun.

1. <u>Carrie's</u> bike is red.

2. <u>Sam's</u> story is about frogs.

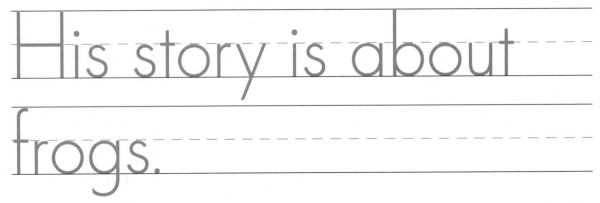

3. <u>Ned's and Tia's</u> house is blue.

4. <u>Ted's and my</u> house is white.

Intervention

Name _____ Date _____

Read the story.

Planting Time

Our town has a garden that we share. Our garden is in the town's park. We plow and rake the ground. We take out large sticks and stones. Then we plan the garden.

In spring, flowers bloom. Around these flowers we plant seeds that will grow food. We plant seeds for tomatoes, beans, cucumbers, and peas.

If we could look underground, we could see how seeds sprout. Sprouts drink water from the ground. Worms and ants dig holes that make the ground better for the plants. These holes let air into the ground.

Sunflowers are gold and brown. Sunflowers tower over the fence in summer. Butterflies and bees swoop around the garden.

Illustrate the setting of the story.

After students have read the story, ask them the following questions. When possible, have students answer by pointing to and reading aloud the answers in the text.

• **What kinds of flowers do you visualize growing in the town garden?** Possible Answer: *I visualize sunflowers and roses growing in the town garden.*

• **Which types of food seeds do they plant?** *The people plant seeds for tomatoes, beans, cucumbers, and peas.*

Name _____ Date _____

Read each clue. Decide which word in the word box answers the question. Write the word on the line.

slice	mice	night	light

1. The opposite of day is **night**.

2. The opposite of dark is **light**.

3. If you do not want a whole pizza, you can buy

just one **slice**.

4. We don't have just one mouse. We have

two **mice**.

Name _____ Date _____

Read each sentence below and look for spelling, punctuation, and capitalization errors. Rewrite the sentence correctly on the line.

1. have you ever visited oakley california

Have you ever visited Oakley, California?

_____

2. raul was born on february 27 1993

Raul was born on February 27, 1993.

_____

3. lucy marcella and tom attend walnut elementary school Lucy, Marcella, and Tom attend

Walnut Elementary School.

_____

4. watch out for that bus coming your way

Watch out for that bus coming your way!

_____

Name _____ Date _____

Name each picture. Write the missing letters to complete the word.

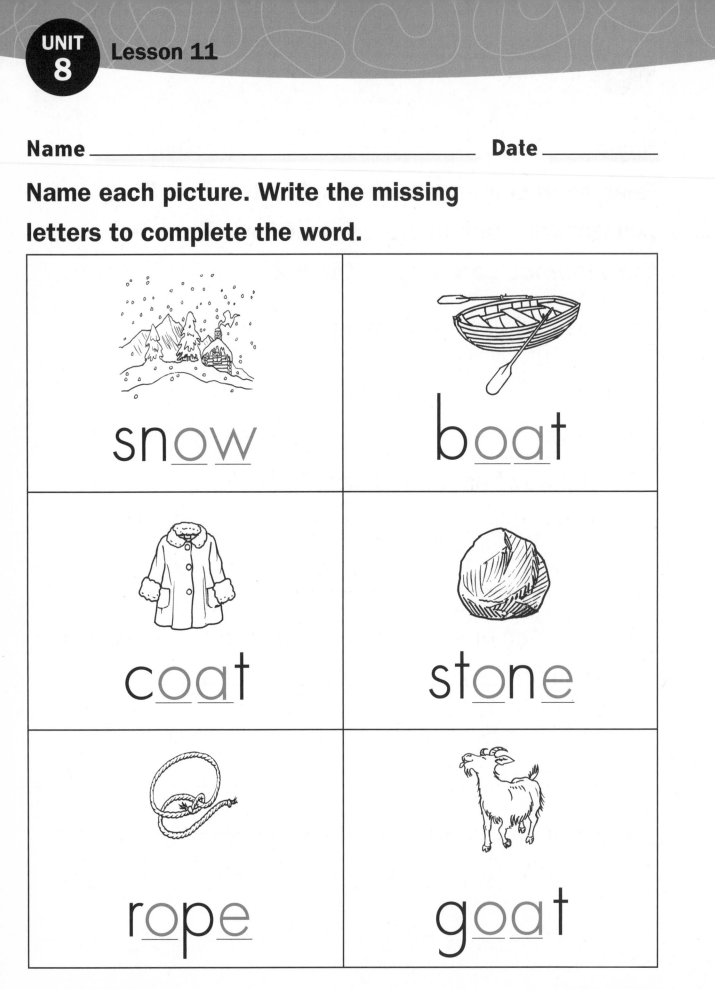

sn<u>ow</u>

b<u>oa</u>t

c<u>oa</u>t

st<u>o</u>n<u>e</u>

r<u>o</u>p<u>e</u>

g<u>oa</u>t

Name _____ Date _____

**The words in the right column are
synonyms for the words in the left
column. Read the words in both columns.
Then, draw lines to connect the words in
the left column with their synonyms in the
right column.**

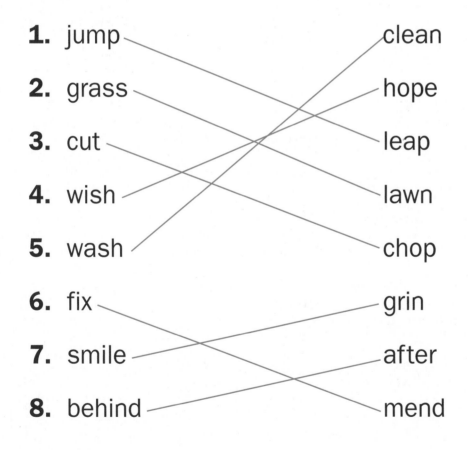

1. jump   clean

2. grass   hope

3. cut   leap

4. wish   lawn

5. wash   chop

6. fix   grin

7. smile   after

8. behind   mend

Name _____ Date _____

Read the following words. Circle the words that have the short o sound.

(cost)   hold

sold   (top)

roll   troll

both   (moth)

(cloth)   gold

fold   ghost

(hot)   (lost)

most   post

(cot)   colt

bold   (doll)

Name _____ **Date** _____

Read the story.

The Harvest

Everyone visits the town square in summer. Children play all around. We work in the garden. But no dogs are allowed!

Sometimes in June, the clouds get dark. We hear loud thunder. Then the garden gets a shower!

We take good care of the ground around the plants.

We take out the weeds. Plants are stronger when they are not crowded by weeds.

At the end of summer, we harvest the food we planted and grew. Our crew works for hours! Then we are surrounded by pounds and pounds of super cucumbers, beans, peas, and tomatoes.

We have a picnic at the town park.

Illustrate an event from the story.

After students have read the story, ask them the following questions. When possible, have students answer by pointing to and reading aloud the answers in the text.

• Do you have a garden? If so, what do you grow? Possible Answers: *I have a garden. I grow herbs.*

• What animals are not allowed at the park? *Dogs are not allowed at the park.*

• What do the people have in the town park during harvest. *People have a picnic.*

Name _____ Date _____

Read the following names of fruits and vegetables. Then write each item in the correct column on the chart.

| carrot | bean | apple | grape | potato |
| peach | plum | pea | melon | beet |

FRUITS	VEGETABLES
apple	carrot
grape	bean
peach	potato
plum	beet
melon	pea

Name _____ Date _____

Read the sentences about getting ready for school. Some sentences are out of place. Rewrite the sentences so that they make sense and are in the correct order.

When my alarm rings, I climb out of bed. Last, I grab my book bag and walk to the bus stop. Then, I brush my teeth and get dressed. Before I leave, my dad gives me money for lunch.

When my alarm goes off, I climb out of bed.

Then, I brush my teeth and get dressed.

Before I leave, my dad gives me money for

lunch. Last, I grab my book bag and walk to

the bus stop.

_____

_____

_____

Name _____ Date _____

Read each of these clues. Choose a word from the box that matches each clue and write it on the line.

mule	**tune**	**cube**
tube	**cute**	

1. This is a cross between a horse and a donkey.

mule

2. It holds toothpaste. tube

3. This is the shape of ice. cube

4. You can hum it. tune

5. Kittens and puppies are this. cute

Intervention

Name _____ **Date** _____

The words in the columns below are antonyms. Read the words in both columns. Draw a line to connect the word in the left column with its antonyms in the right column.

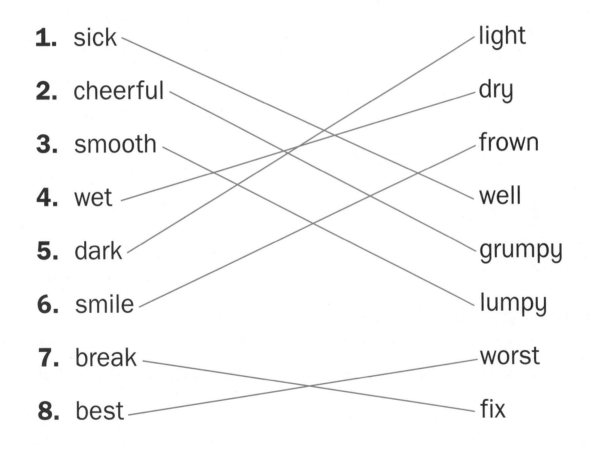

1. sick   light

2. cheerful   dry

3. smooth   frown

4. wet   well

5. dark   grumpy

6. smile   lumpy

7. break   worst

8. best   fix

Name _____ Date _____

Read the sentences. Add words to each sentence to tell how, when, or where the action happened. Rewrite your new sentences on the lines below.

1. Lena likes to play. *Where?*

Possible answer: Lena likes to play outside.

2. Austin sang a song. *How?*

Possible answer: Austin sang a song loudly.

3. It is Tina's last day of school. *When?*

Possible answer: Tina's last day of school is June 3.

_____

Name _____ **Date** _____

Read the story.

Luke's Garden

Luke and his mom grew roses in their garden.

Their garden had beets and turnips, too.

Rabbits came to chew on the new leaves.

Luke shooed away the rude rabbits.

His mom threw away the weeds.

The birds came to their garden in winter and flew away in June.

Luke and his new buddy Drew got roses for their teacher.

"These take my breath away!" their teacher told Luke and Drew.

Illustrate the setting of the story.

After students have read the story, ask them the following questions. When possible, have students answer by pointing to and reading aloud the answers in the text.

- What color(s) do you see in your mind when the story talks about roses? Possible Answer: *I see pink and red.*
- Which animal comes and chews on the new leaves? *Rabbits chew on the new leaves.*
- When do the birds come to Luke's garden? *The birds come to the garden in the winter.*

Name _____ **Date** _____

Read one word in each line. Have students circle the word you read. (The word to read is circled in magenta.)

1. red   road   ride   (run)

2. and   all   (any)   at

3. they   the   (them)   there

4. (of)   on   off   or

5. can   cat   car   (care)

6. (blue)   blow   black   bike

7. go   to   no   (new)

8. away   (about)   above   alone

Name _____ Date _____

Rewrite each sentence on the line. Make sure you form the letters correctly.

1. Brian plays the trumpet in the Rosewood Elementary School band.

Brian plays the trumpet in the Rosewood

Elementary School band.

2. Before making a sandwich, Raul got a plate.

Before making a sandwich, Raul got a plate.

_____

3. Britney and Robin walk down Renner Street.

Britney and Robin walk down Renner Street.

_____

Check to make sure students have correctly formed all the letters, with an emphasis on capital letters B and R.

Name _____ Date _____

Read these words. Circle the two words in each row that have the same long-vowel sound.

1. (beak)   break   (heap)

2. (seen)   head   (green)

3. (home)   (roam)   come

4. (most)   cost   (host)

5. (wait)   (came)   walk

6. rain   (white)   (right)

7. (new)   (soon)   so

8. great   (heat)   (feet)

Name _____ Date _____

Read the pairs of words at the left and the contractions at the right. Draw lines to match the words in the left column with their contractions in the right column.

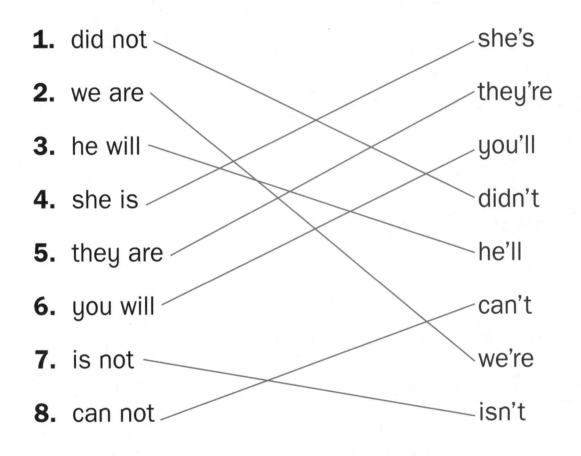

1. did not   she's

2. we are   they're

3. he will   you'll

4. she is   didn't

5. they are   he'll

6. you will   can't

7. is not   we're

8. can not   isn't

Name _____ Date _____

Read each sentence. Write the two words that make up the contraction in each sentence.

1. Holly isn't here today.

   __is__   __not__

2. She's staying at home.

   __she__   __is__

3. She wasn't feeling well.

   __was__   __not__

4. So she didn't come to school.

   __did__   __not__

5. I think she'll be back tomorrow.

   __she__   __will__

Name _____ **Date** _____

Read the story.

Dee's Trees

Once there was a girl named Dee. She found a plant and put it in the ground. It grew. She grew, too. She turned into a woman, and the plant turned into a tree.

Dee had a small boy, and he grew. He turned into a man. The small tree turned into a big tree. Soon the man was a father.

He had a small girl. One day the small girl found a plant, and she put it in the ground. It will grow, too.

Illustrate a character from the story.

After students have read the story, ask them the following questions. When possible, have students answer by pointing to and reading aloud the answers in the text.

- How much time does it take for a person and a plant to grow? *It takes a long time for a person to grow. It can take a long time for a plant to grow, too.*
- What did the plant turn into? *The plant turned into a tree.*
- What did the small girl find at the end of the story? *The small girl found a plant.*

Name _____ Date _____

Rewrite the following words paying close attention to forming the capital letters O, C, T, H, B, and R correctly.

1. October   October

2. Colorado   Colorado

3. Herman   Herman

4. Tuesday   Tuesday

5. Baltimore   Baltimore

6. Rachel   Rachel

Check to make sure students have correctly formed all the letters, with an emphasis on capital letters O, C, T, H, B, and R.

Name _____ **Date** _____

Read the words with students. Have them circle the words in which *ea* stands for /ē/.

1. (leave)   heavy

2. (teach)   head

3. breath   great

4. (beast)   (please)

5. bread   pleasure

6. meadow   measure

7. (reach)   (measles)

8. ready   (heal)

9. (leader)   (easy)

10. (beneath)   steady

Name _____ Date _____

Read the words in the box. Read each sentence. Write the word on the line that completes each sentence. You should use each word only once.

puppies	**dirty**	**hurry**	**pets**	**wheat**	**wet**

1. Fern has to ___hurry___ or she will be late.

2. Jack took his ___pets___ to the vet.

3. The ___dirty___ dog needs a bath.

4. You'll get ___wet___ if you walk in the rain.

5. Henry loves ___wheat___ bread.

6. Kevin's dog had ten ___puppies___.

Name _____ **Date** _____

Read each present-tense verb with students. Then have them circle the correct past-tense form.

1. do   (did)   doed

2. go   gid   (went)

3. jump   jumpped   (jumped)

4. hum   (hummed)   humed

5. try   tryed   (tried)

6. play   (played)   plaied

7. stand   standed   (stood)

8. hand   (handed)   hood

9. see   seed   (saw)

10. free   (freed)   fraw

Name _____ Date _____

Read the story.

A Home for Boots

Tim thinks Boots is the best dog in the world. But Tim does not know that Boots is not just his dog.

When Tim goes to school, Boots waits for the bus with him. When Tim gets off the bus, Boots is on the sidewalk. When Tim goes to the playground, Boots goes, too. Boots goes down the slide and rides on the swings with Tim.

Each night Tim asks, "May Boots sleep in my room?" And each night Tim's mom and dad say, "No."

So Tim sends Boots out to the yard. The dog sneaks out of the yard. Then Boots goes to the firehouse.

When the man at the firehouse sees Boots, he says, "Hi, Rags. Have you come home to sleep?"

And Boots wags his tail and jumps into his bed!

Illustrate an event from the story.

Ask students the first question before they complete the story. Have students read the story. Then ask them the remaining questions. When possible, have students answer by pointing to and reading aloud the answers in the text.

- **What does Boots do at the playground?** *Boots goes down the slide and rides the swing with Tim.*
- **Where do you think Boots will sleep?** Possible Answer: *I think Boots will sleep in Tim's bed.*
- **What does the man at the firehouse call Boots?** *The man at the firehouse calls him Rags.*

Name _____ **Date** _____

Look at the two pictures below. Use the chart to tell how the pictures are alike and how they are different.

Different (Contrast)	Same (Compare)	Different (Contrast)
YARD A	**YARD A & B**	**YARD B**
swing in the tree	grass	bird feeder in tree
wading pool	trees	flower bed
fence	picnic table	hedge

Name _____ Date _____

Part 1

Read the verbs. Rewrite the verbs by adding *-ed* to each word to form the past tense.

1. stop   _____stopped_____

2. thank   _____thanked_____

3. shout   _____shouted_____

4. like   _____liked_____

5. worry   _____worried_____

6. watch   _____watched_____

Part 2

Write a sentence using one of the past-tense verbs from above.

Answers will vary. Accept sentences in
which verb was correctly used.

Name _____ Date _____

Name each picture. Write the missing letter to complete the word.

1. snail

2. clock

3. gloves

4. bread

5. twig

6. price

Name _____ Date _____

Read each past-tense verb. Write the present-tense form of the same verb on the line.

1. came _____come_____

2. drew _____draw_____

3. sat _____sit_____

4. jumped _____jump_____

5. saw _____see_____

6. made _____make_____

7. told _____tell_____

8. looked _____look_____

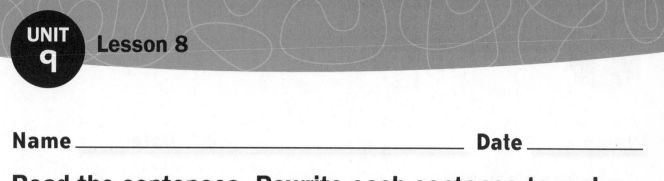

Name _____ **Date** _____

Read the sentences. Rewrite each sentence to make it tell about something that already happened.

1. Carrie rides her bike.

   Carrie rode her bike.

2. Sam writes a story.

   Sam wrote a story.

3. Ned tells a joke.

   Ned told a joke.

4. Stacey carries the books.

   Stacey carried the books.

Name _____ **Date** _____

Read the story.

A New Home

Kelly stood on the sidewalk and looked at her new house. She was not happy. She was in a new town. All her friends lived far away.

A girl came out of the house across the street. She waved and called to Kelly, "Are you moving in?"

"Yes," Kelly said.

"I'm Dina," said the girl. "I'm glad you're here. Come over later." She waved again and went back inside.

Kelly smiled. She felt a lot better.

Illustrate an event from the story.

After students have read the story, ask them the following questions. When possible, have students answer by pointing to and reading aloud the answers in the text.

- How does the author explain why Kelly is unhappy? Possible Answer: *The author says Kelly is new in town and her friends live far away.*
- Who invited Kelly to come over? *Dina invited Kelly to come over.*
- How did Kelly feel after she met Dina? Possible Answer: *Kelly smiled and felt a lot better.*

Name _____ Date _____

Read each set of three words. Rewrite the words on the lines in alphabetical order.

1. wood   <u>brick</u>

2. brick   <u>stone</u>

3. stone   <u>wood</u>

4. roof   <u>floor</u>

5. walls   <u>roof</u>

6. floor   <u>walls</u>

7. window   <u>door</u>

8. door   <u>porch</u>

9. porch   <u>window</u>

Name _____ Date _____

Read each topic and the ideas that follow it. Identify the idea that does not match the topic and circle it.

Topic: Parts of a House

Walls   Floor

Roof   Windows

Cars   Doors

Topic: Building a House

Make the foundation.   Build the walls.

Put on the roof.   Birds build nests.

Put in the windows.   Put down the floor.

Name _____ **Date** _____

Name each picture. Write the letters that complete each word.

1.

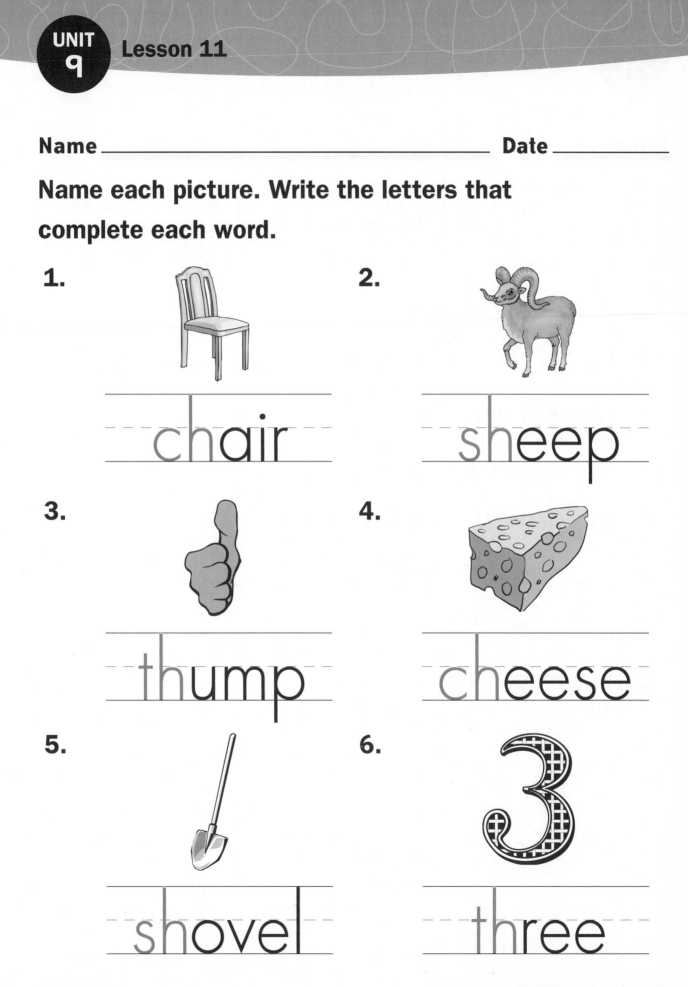

chair

2.

sheep

3.

thump

4.

cheese

5.

shovel

6.

three

Name _____ **Date** _____

Read the sentences with students. Have students decide if the sentence tells about something that is happening now, something that already happened, or something that is going to happen. They should write N for *Now* if it tells about something that is happening now. They should write B for *Before* if it tells about something that already happened. They should write L for *Later* if it tells about something that is going to happen.

1. William is hungry. _____N_____

2. He ate breakfast three hours ago. _____B_____

3. Now it is time for lunch. _____N_____

4. William will get his lunch. _____L_____

5. He will go to the lunch room. _____L_____

6. He looks in his lunch box. _____N_____

7. Mom gave him soup. _____B_____

8. She made him a sandwich. _____B_____

Name _____ Date _____

Part 1: Read the steps for washing your hair. Number the steps from 1 to 5 to show the correct order.

___5___ Dry your hair with a towel.

___2___ Put shampoo in your hair.

___3___ Make it sudsy.

___1___ Get your hair wet.

___4___ Rinse out the suds.

Part 2: Read the steps for checking out a book from the library. Number the steps from 1 to 5 to show the correct order.

___3___ Take the book to the desk.

___2___ Find a book you like.

___1___ Find the children's books.

___4___ Get out your library card.

___5___ Check out the book.

Name _____ **Date** _____

Read the story.

Zoomer and Boomer

My name is Zoomer.

I am going to see my granddad, Boomer.

I came at noon.

Boomer was at the bus stop to meet me.

He scooped me up in his arms.

I am glad I came here.

Boomer's home is shaped like the moon.

It has a funny roof.

When I came, there was a cup and a spoon for me.

I like the food here.

I like my room, too.

I go to sleep when the birds start to hoot.

llustrate an event from the story.

After students have read the story, ask them the following questions. When possible, have students answer by pointing to and reading aloud the answers in the text.

• **What color do you visualize when you read about Boomer's moon-shaped house?** Possible Answer: *I visualize a yellow shape like a smile.*

• **How does Zoomer get to Boomer's house?** *Zoomer takes a bus to get to Boomer's house.*

• **When does Zoomer go to sleep?** *Zoomer goes to sleep when the birds start to hoot.*

Name _____ **Date** _____

Read one word in each line. Have students circle the word you read. (The word to read is circled in magenta.)

1. (would)   why   which   where

2. same   (some)   said   says

3. yoke   your   yikes   (yellow)

4. (they)   them   then   there

5. (them)   thought   though   throw

6. went   want   were   (we're)

7. alone   (away)   also   alike

8. (very)   ever   even   except

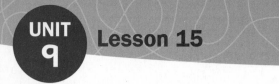

Name _____ Date _____

Read the sentences. Rewrite each sentence to make it tell about something that will happen in the future.

1. Ali is feeding the dog.

Ali will feed the dog.

2. Dad walks the dog.

Dad will walk the dog.

3. I pet the dog.

I will pet the dog.

4. Mom brushes the dog.

Mom will brush the dog.

5. The dog looks great.

The dog will look great.

Name _____ Date _____

Read these words with students. Have them circle the two words in each row that have the r-controlled vowels.

1. (shirt)   (birch)   have

2. break   (lurk)   (burst)

3. mole   (purr)   (stir)

4. (were)   (cure)   come

5. (burnt)   eight   (torn)

6. (person)   (skirt)   pushy

7. (snort)   (curt)   know

8. (lurk)   (her)   story

Name _____ Date _____

Name each picture. Complete the picture names by writing a vowel and the letter *r* on the line.

1.

car

2.

curl

3.

dirt

4.

pearl

5.

finger

6.

shirt

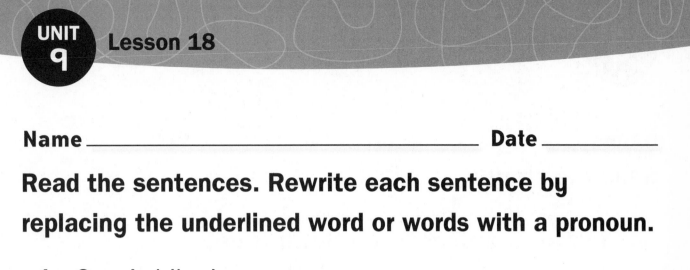
Name _____ Date _____

Read the sentences. Rewrite each sentence by replacing the underlined word or words with a pronoun.

1. <u>Suzy's</u> bike is green.

   <u>Her bike is green.</u>

2. <u>Matt's</u> bike is green, too.

   <u>His bike is green, too.</u>

3. <u>The bikes</u> were side by side.

   <u>They were side by side.</u>

4. <u>Matt</u> took <u>Suzy's</u> bike.

   <u>He took her bike.</u>

5. <u>Suzy</u> took <u>Matt's</u> bike.

   <u>She took his bike.</u>

6. How did <u>Matt and Suzy</u> know <u>Matt and Suzy's</u> mistake?

   <u>How did they know their mistake?</u>

Name _____ Date _____

Read the story.

Little Hen Sees Something New

Little Hen lived on a farm. She lived in a nice barn. One day she wanted to see something new. So Little Hen left the farm.

Little Hen saw something new. She saw a fox on a rock. The fox saw her too.

"Time for lunch!" said the fox.

"Time to fly!" said Little Hen. Then she flew into a tree.

Little Hen waited until the fox left.

"That was new," said Little Hen. "But old is best." Then she ran home fast.

Illustrate the setting of the story.

After students have read the story, ask them the following questions. When possible, have students answer by pointing to and reading aloud the answers in the text.

- Little Hen wanted to see something new. What new things would you like to see? Possible Answers: *I would like to see a new movie.*
- What did Little Hen see when she left the farm? *Little Hen saw a fox.*
- How did Little Hen get away from the fox? *Little Hen got away from the fox by flying into a tree.*

Name _____ Date _____

Read one word in each line. Have students circle the word you read. (The word to read is circled in magenta.)

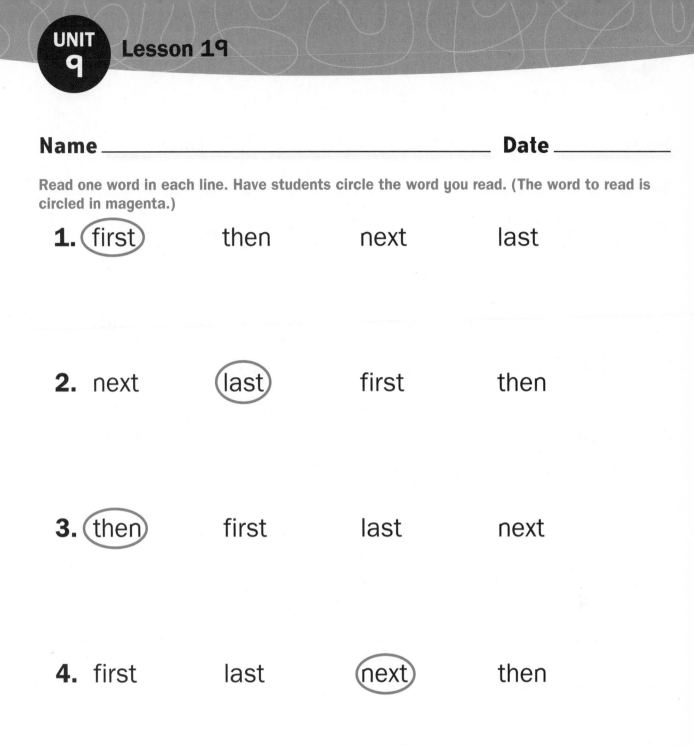

1. first   then   next   last

2. next   last   first   then

3. then   first   last   next

4. first   last   next   then

Name _____ Date _____

Read the sentences. Rewrite each sentence replacing the underlined words with the correct pronoun or possessive pronoun from the box.

him	them	their	they	our	her

1. Katy and Tim are going to the zoo.

  They are going to the zoo.

2. My family's car is in the driveway.

  Our car is in the driveway.

3. Those books belong to Mrs. Grove's class.

  Those books belong to them.

4. Mike and Seth's baseball was lost.

  Their baseball was lost.

5. It is Ann's cat.

  It is her cat.

6. Mrs. Sesser's kids played kickball with Jim.

  Mrs. Sesser's kids played kickball with him.

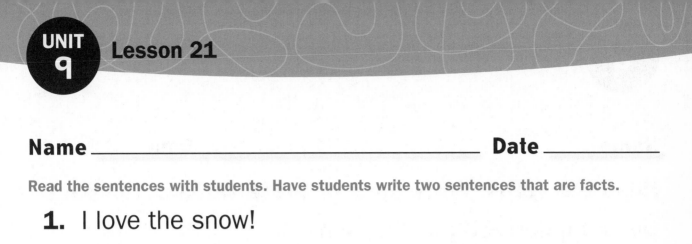

Name _____ **Date** _____

Read the sentences with students. Have students write two sentences that are facts.

1. I love the snow!

a. <u>Answers will vary. It is cold outside.</u>

b. <u>It is winter.</u>

2. Kent is a good student.

a. <u>Answers will vary. He is going to read a book.</u>

b. <u>He is going to study.</u>

Name _____ **Date** _____

Read the verbs. Write each of these verbs in the past tense by correctly adding –*ed*.

1. stare ___stared___ **2.** trade ___traded___

3. hurry ___hurried___ **4.** try ___tried___

5. bury ___buried___ **6.** change ___changed___

7. use ___used___ **8.** carry ___carried___

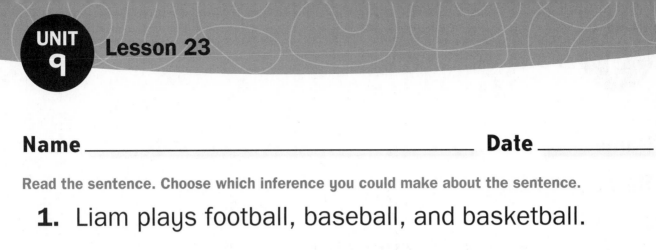

Name _____ **Date** _____

Read the sentence. Choose which inference you could make about the sentence.

1. Liam plays football, baseball, and basketball.

  a. Liam is good at many different sports.

  b. Liam does not like math.

2. Jenna is a good student.

  a. Jenna studies a lot.

  b. Jenna plays chess.

3. It is raining outside.

  a. It will rain tomorrow.

  b. I should take my umbrella.

4. I am hungry!

  a. I watched TV last night.

  b. I didn't eat lunch.

Name _____ Date _____

Read the story.

Space Station Home

Today will be fun. Some people are coming to our house!

I get up early. I float to the bathroom. I brush my teeth. Then I float to the kitchen.

Mom wants to make a special meal. She has to be careful. If the food gets loose, it might drift away.

Dad is now at the gate. The shuttle is here! Two people in space suits come down the ramp.

"Grandma! Grandpa!" I call and wave. "Welcome to our home in space!"

Illustrate the setting of the story.

After students have read the story, ask them the following questions. When possible, have students answer by pointing to and reading aloud the answers in the text.

- **What questions do you have about living in space? Possible Answer:** *I wonder how you stay in bed if you float everywhere in space.*
- **What does the main character do after brushing his or her teeth?** *After brushing his or her teeth, the main character floats into the kitchen.*
- **Who came to visit?** *Grandma and Grandpa came to visit.*

Name _____ **Date** _____

Say the words. Have students fill in the missing letters to complete each word. Then have students write the word in past-tense form.

1. b __a__ k __e__   ____baked____

2. t ____ie____   ____tied____

3. n ____a____ p   ____napped____

4. g ____e____ t   ____got____

5. b ____oi____ l   ____boiled____

6. ____sh____ ine   ____shined____

7. fa ____ll____   ____fell____

8. st ____ir____   ____stirred____

Name _____ Date _____

Read the words below. If the word sounds like the /oo/ in *book*, write the word in the left column. If the word sounds like the /o͞o/ in *proof*, write the word in the right column.

blew   clue   nook   rule   cook   look

book	proof
nook	blew
cook	clue
look	rule

Name _____ **Date** _____

Read the words with students. Have them circle the words in which oo stands for /oo/.

tooth

booth

(good)

stoop

(stood)

fool

tool

(book)

(look)

(shook)

school

noon

(wood)

(foot)

shoot

scoot

(roof)

proof

(brook)

(took)

Name _____ Date _____

Read the words in the first column of the chart. For each word, choose a word from the box that has the same meaning and one that has the opposite meaning. Write the words in the appropriate columns.

fib   lift   lower   piece   start   truth   whole   quit

Word	Means the Same	Means the Opposite
lie	fib	truth
raise	lift	lower
part	piece	whole
stop	quit	start

Name _____ **Date** _____

Read the story.

The Knitting Knight

A knight mopes around the moat, knitting.

He wants to go out and wander about.

He wants to stroll around the river and fish for trout.

He may not go out and about.

He is the knight on lookout.

He knits, and he mopes.

He wants to climb around on grassy slopes.

The knight may not wander about the town.

He sits and knits and keeps his vow.

The knight is proud to keep his land safe.

Illustrate an event from the story.

After students have read the story, ask them the following questions. When possible, have students answer by pointing to and reading aloud the answers in the text.

- What might you ask the knight about his job? Possible Answer: *How do you keep the land safe?*
- What does the knight do while on lookout? *The knight knits and mopes while on lookout.*
- What would the knight like to be doing instead of being on lookout? *The knight would like to be climbing grassy slopes instead of being on lookout.*

Name _____ **Date** _____

The list of authors below is in alphabetical order. Write the three authors' names at the top of the list on the line where each belongs.

Mem Fox	James Marshall	Dr. Seuss

Marc Brown

Eric Carle

Tomi DePaola

<u>Mem Fox</u>

Gail Gibbons

Kevin Henkes

Leo Lionni

<u>James Marshall</u>

Robert Munsch

Barbara Park

Cynthia Rylant

<u>Dr. Seuss</u>

Name _____ Date _____

Practice writing each of the words on the lines.

Then, rewrite the sentence making sure you form the

letters correctly.

1. Vermont   _____ Vermont _____

2. Wednesday   _____ Wednesday _____

3. Wilson   _____ Wilson _____

4. Virginia   _____ Virginia _____

Wayne went to Vermont to visit Vanessa, Vance, and Webster.

Wayne went to Vermont to visit Vanessa,
Vance, and Webster.

Check to make sure students have correctly formed all the letters, with an emphasis on capital letters *V* and *W*.

Name _____ **Date** _____

Read aloud the following words. Have students circle the words that have the /ow/ sound.

(cow)   blown

grow   (brown)

(how)   shown

low   (down)

(now)   grown

row   (frown)

show   should

snow   (shout)

(wow)   (proud)

(loud)   could

Name _____ Date _____

Read each sentence. Write T if the sentence is a "telling sentence" or A if the sentence is an "asking sentence."

1. Where are my boots? _____ A

2. I can't find them anywhere. _____ T

3. Did you look in the closet? _____ A

4. Did you look by the door? _____ A

5. I wore them yesterday. _____ T

6. I left them on the mat. _____ T

7. What does the dog have? _____ A

8. That's one of my boots. _____ T

9. He's carrying it around. _____ T

10. Where is the other one? _____ A

Name _____ Date _____

Read the following words. Circle the words that have the/oi/sound.

(annoy)   (joy)

happy   (boy)

made   (boil)

(hoist)   cry

baby   (oil)

Name _____ **Date** _____

Read the following sentences. On the line after the sentence, write I for imperative sentence (a command or request), T for telling sentence, A for asking sentence, or S for strong feeling sentence. Then, on the line after the sentence, change the sentence as it asks you to do and rewrite it on the line.

1. I like Wednesdays. _T_

strong feeling sentence: _I love Wednesdays!_

2. Should you play in the street? _A_

imperative sentence: _Don't play in the street!_

3. Pick up my pencil now! _I_

asking sentence: _Would you please pick up my pencil?_

4. I love my dog so much! _S_

telling sentence: _I like my dog._

Name _____ **Date** _____

Read each sentence. Write the word that has a word ending added to it and write it on the line.

1. Tony likes his dog. _____likes_____

2. Lauren talked to her mom. _____talked_____

3. Some think an airplane is safer than a car.
   _____safer_____

4. Alan is a lucky person. _____lucky_____

5. Camille has the neatest handwriting.
   _____neatest_____

6. Julie likes carrots. _____likes_____

Name _____ **Date** _____

Read each of these words. For each word, write the base word.

1. hummed   _____hum_____

2. funniest   _____funny_____

3. hurried   _____hurry_____

4. dancing   _____dance_____

5. escaped   _____escape_____

6. skipping   _____skip_____

7. raced   _____race_____

8. practicing   _____practice_____

9. noisier   _____noisy_____

10. noticed   _____notice_____

11. smiling   _____smile_____

12. bravest   _____brave_____

Name _____ Date _____

Write these five book titles where they belong in alphabetical order.

Eloise   **Piggie Pie!**   **Too Many Frogs**
Library Lion   **Ruby the Copycat**

Are You My Mother?

Bootsie Barker Bites

_____Eloise_____

Harold and the Purple Crayon

Henry and Mudge

____Library Lion____

____Piggie Pie!____

Rotten Ralph

Ruby the Copycat

Scaredy Squirrel

Too Many Frogs

Name _____ Date _____

Read the story.

Noises in the Night

Nia went to her grandmother's house. There was a room just for her. She liked that. There was a big bed. She liked that, too. But that night she heard noises, and she didn't like that.

She put on the light. Nobody was there. She put out the light. But the noises went on.

"Go away," she said.

Still the noises went on. Nia bravely stepped into the hall. There was her noise. It was a big clock. It went "tick, tock" all the time. "You're not scary," Nia laughed at the clock.

Illustrate an event from the story.

Ask students the first question before they complete the story. Then have them answer the remaining questions. When possible, have students answer by pointing to and reading aloud the answers in the text.

• After reading the title and the first half of the story, do you think Nia will face her fear? Possible Answer: *I think Nia will face her fear.*

• How were the bed and the clock alike? Possible Answer: *Both the bed and the clock were big.*

• What did Nia do when she realized the clock was making the noises? *Nia laughed when she realized the clock was making the noises.*

Name _____ Date _____

**Read the story. Answer each question with an X.
Follow the directions under each question.**

Pam rubbed her hands while <u>looking up and down</u>
<u>the street.</u> She pulled her coat around her and put
her hands in her pockets. Sitting on the bench, Pam
shivered and waited.

1. Where is Pam? inside ___ outside _X_

   **Draw a line under the words in the story that tell
   you this.**

2. What was it like outside? cold _X_ warm ___

   **Draw circles around the words in the story that
   tell you this.**

Name _____ **Date** _____

Read the words below. Choose a prefix or suffix from the word box to change the word. Write the new word on the line.

un-	-er	-est	-ed	-ing

1. nice   most nice   _nicest_

2. walk   present tense _walking_

3. fast   more fast   _faster_

4. call   past tense   _called_

5. pretty most pretty _prettiest_

6. selfish not selfish _unselfish_

7. smart more smart _smarter_

8. tied   not tied   _untied_

Name _____ **Date** _____

Read the words. Write the base word from each one on the line.

1. peaceful _____peace_____

2. useful _____use_____

3. forgetful _____forget_____

4. colorful _____color_____

5. careful _____care_____

6. cheerful _____cheer_____

7. sadness _____sad_____

8. brightness _____bright_____

9. happiness _____happy_____

10. silliness _____silly_____

Name _____ Date _____

Read each set of words. Circle the two words in each row that rhyme.

1. grown (crown) (brown)

2. slower (shower) (tower)

3. bowl (howl) (prowl)

4. (shown) clown (thrown)

5. (wowed) slowed (crowd)

6. (showed) (mowed) allowed

7. (gown) (frown) flown

8. (rower) power (lower)

Name _____ Date _____

Read the sentences. Underline the contraction in the sentence. Then write the two words that make up the contraction on the lines.

1. Mary <u>won't</u> tell me.

___will___   ___not___

2. <u>She's</u> in my class.

___She___   ___is___

3. I <u>wouldn't</u> eat pickles.

___would___   ___not___

4. He <u>doesn't</u> like trains.

___does___   ___not___

5. The chicken <u>can't</u> fly.

___can___   ___not___

6. <u>I'll</u> be at home.

___I___   ___will___

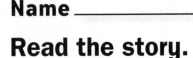
Name _____ Date _____

Read the story.

Big Prints!

Gus is at the log bridge.

Gus spots big, big prints in the snow!

Gus spots prints at the flagpole. What could make such big prints? Something big? Something scary?

On the edge of the path, Gus spots prints.

Then Gus spots Meg. She is walking in the snow.

She has snowshoes on her feet. Meg has big, big prints!

Illustrate a character from the story.

After students have read the story, ask them the following questions. When possible, have students answer by pointing to and reading aloud the answers in the text.

- What do you think the big prints look like? Possible Answer: *The big prints look like big bear footprints.*
- Where is Gus when he first spots the big prints? *Gus is at the log bridge when he first spots the big prints.*
- Who is making the big prints? *Meg is making the big prints with her snowshoes.*

Name _____ Date _____

Use the words in the word box below to correctly complete the sentences and write them on the lines. Use each word only once.

---

underneath thrill solo sneaking usually
clumsy excitement peeking match suggest

---

1. My little brother looks ___clumsy___ because he is just learning to walk.

2. Do you think these shoes will ___match___ my dress?

3. Will you play a piano ___solo___ at the concert tonight?

4. I think roller coasters are a ___thrill___!

5. We ___usually___ go to the park on Sundays.

6. Henry saw the mice ___sneaking___ into the attic.

7. Where do you ___suggest___ we find the definition of the word?

8. My dog hides his treats ___underneath___ the table.

9. The scared child was ___peeking___ out from underneath the blanket.

10. The party in Mrs. Campbell's classroom caused a lot of ___excitement___.